NEW YORK
NY 10047/48

The Public Process of Rebuilding
the World Trade Center after
September 11, 2001

CHRISTOPH FAULHABER

KERBER
EDITION YOUNG ART

imprint

*New York, NY 10047/48 used to be the zip code
of the World Trade Center, Tower I and II*

Editor, Author:
Christoph Faulhaber
Copyediting:
Katrin Günther
Translation into English:
Michael Scuffil, Josephine Cordero Sapién

Cover: Ground Zero, C. Faulhaber, 2002
Img. 8, p. 34: National Oceanic and Atmospheric Administration (NOAA). Image taken by NOAA's Cessna Citation Jet on Sept. 23, 2001 from an altitude of 3,300 feet using a Leica/LH systems RC30 camera.

This book is kindly supported by
Freie und Hansestadt Hamburg
(Behörde für Kultur, Sport und Medien)
Schirn Kunsthalle, Frankfurt
artfinder | Galerie Mathias Güntner, Hamburg
and Kerber Verlag, Bielefeld/Leipzig/Berlin

Printed and published by
Kerber Verlag, Bielefeld
Windelsbleicher Str. 166–170
33659 Bielefeld
Deutschland /Germany
Tel. +49 (0) 5 21 9 50 08 10
Fax +49 (0) 5 21 9 50 08 88
info@kerberverlag.com
www.kerberverlag.com

Kerber, US Distribution
D. A. P., Distributed Art Publishers, Inc.
155 Sixth Avenue, 2nd Floor
New York, NY 10013
Tel. +1 212 6 27 19 99
Fax +1 212 6 27 94 84

Freie und Hansestadt Hamburg

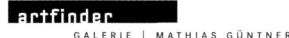
GALERIE | MATHIAS GÜNTNER

This book is a reprint of the first issue, published in 2002, according to Faulhaber's diploma thesis at the Hochschule für Bildende Künste Hamburg. Mentors: Prof. Jane Sörensen and Prof. Lambert Rosenbusch. ISBN 3–00–009888–7

It is published on the occasion of the exhibition "Playing the City 2" at Schirn Kunsthalle, Frankfurt, curated by Matthias Ulrich.

The Deutsche Nationalbibliothek holds a record of this publication in the Deutsche Nationalbibliografie; detailed bibliographical data can be found under: http://dnb.d-nb.de.

ISBN 978-3-86678-454-3

Printed in Germany

table of contents

preface

This is the reprint of the book that was originally published in 2002. The text has been shortened and translated into English. Due to the time shift, some temporary and historical relations have become unclear but have been kept because the original observation was bound to its historical experience.

Today's perspective has rendered the reprint necessary, firstly, because the book presents an arguable claim to the ongoing debates in the aesthetic and sociopolitical domains. Secondly, because this work allows for understanding of the broader range of my whole work and its underlying artistic conception. Thirdly, the first edition is meanwhile unavailable.

Trying to outline the stakes of this book, I would propose to conceive of the unexpected and sudden emptiness in Downtown Manhattan as a *public space*. Publicness or the shared spatial and temporal experience of a civitas and community was described in two independent approaches by urban design expert Dieter Läpple and art historian Nicolas Bourriaud in the 1990s. While Dieter Läpple coined the notion of a *relational space concept*, Nicolas Bourriaud developed an inclusive paradigm for contemporary art production called *relational aesthetics*: creating space through shared action and generating form through spatial experience, temporal encounter and social structure.

This book is about both the potentials and chances as well as the limited possibilities of this ethic-aesthetic approach.

Christoph Faulhaber
Shenzhen, 2010

I cannot remember an event that hit me with such force as the images of 9/11. To me, as to the Americans, it felt like it was "the first attack on home soil." But then the experience dissipated into the metaphysical: the talking began, the discussions, the explanations, the event's instrumentalization and its transposition into the reality of any subjective rationale.

The challenge of the images evokes the cultural production of images that face up to this challenge. What are the cultural and artistic strategies that act and react in this *horror vacui*? What concepts of design and aesthetics for the inevitably necessary future of Ground Zero can develop in an emotional and political climate in which such extremes have been generated?

When I arrived in New York in early 2002 the comparisons with the debate in Germany about the reconstruction of Berlin's historic center were at the heart of these questions: the Berlin City Palace, the Memorial to the Murdered Jews of Europe, Potsdamer Platz and the Jewish Museum. Another question that arose was how this wrestling for design, between symbolic form and historically authentic identity, could be applied to the plans for a new World Trade Center.

Over the course of my work and stay in New York my interest was focused on the movement and energy of the public process. Observations revealed that a communitarian authority had developed in this early stage, which took on the task of coping with the event and its consequences. In search of relevance and authenticity I had the feeling that the public participation could be the only adequate reaction to the challenge; to the challenge of a situation in which people talked about an "attack on the civilized world", "terror against America", the "clash of civilizations" and "war on terror".

The unparalleled efforts of thousands expressed the wrestling for a consensus amidst conflicting interests, and is this wrestling not the purest form of democracy? Future developments will show whether this assessment, which is both political and aesthetic, represents a promise fulfilled or a theoretical ideal.

This work is a tribute to the process and the role of the public. It is a monument-in-writing to the process. In addition this study provides an insight into the complicated structures, and an extensive collection of information about the process determining the future of Ground Zero.

After several works in the context of public art, public sphere and social sculpture it seemed an obvious choice to me to address the situation in New York by approaching it as a socio-critical conceptualization in the contentious area of contemporary architecture. As a result of the thematic and temporal dimensions the present study can only be called incomplete and provisional, a fragment in the weave of collective and global observations.

I am indebted to the initiative *New York New Visions*, whose work has a central position in my observation, not just because of its significance, but also because I myself had the privilege of contributing to this initiative for several months.

Christoph Faulhaber
Hamburg, 2002

introduction

We will rebuild. We are going to come out of this stronger than before, politically stronger, economically stronger. The skyline will be made whole again.
Mayor Rudi Giuliani, Sep. 2001

As a symbol of America's resolve, my administration will work with Congress, and these two leaders, to show the world that we will rebuild New York City.
President George W. Bush, Sep. 2001

reconstruction

As a result of changing political systems, destruction caused by war and territorial shifts, the development of European cities has been shaped by continuing upheavals and new beginnings. By contrast, the development of American cities has experienced flowing change and continuation. After September 11 America faced the challenge of doing justice to the historic dimension of a place, albeit not for the first time, but this time with an awareness of the unknown implications and significant responsibility. The plan was to compensate for the fear of a caesura in the linear development with power and threat scenarios in foreign and domestic policy. However, the much-quoted phrase "Nothing will be the same again!" spreads a sense of unease because discontinuity produces insecurity.

It is for this reason that so many American politicians, architects and town planners voiced opinions in line with those of George W. Bush and Rudi Giuliani shortly after September 11, opinions that focused on rebuilding the World Trade Center: "Whatever they take down, we'll rebuild", Philip Johnson – "We should not move back from that point. We cannot retreat", Peter Eisenman – "We need new buildings that are an even greater symbol of New York than what was there before", Richard Meier.

the palace

The gesture of imitating or even copying destroyed buildings in their reconstruction is interpreted as making a politically symbolic statement. In the discussion about the rebuilding of Berlin's City Palace both sides use their own understanding of history and authenticity in their arguments. The proponents of rebuilding the City Palace are accused of revisionism, of seeking to restore the past while ignoring the last century, while their opponents are accused of a raised-finger mentality and of placing too much political emphasis on the past hundred years. What both sides have in common is the connotation of history in the sense of documentation and education. However, the one side favors a historical city-planning ensemble, while the other wants to maintain a cityscape in the process of historical changes.

The fundamental difference lies in the understanding of city and cityscape. On the one hand there is a kind of *diachronic* cityscape, in which a stage-set-like architectural sculpture communicates certain historical ideas and ideals, and on the other hand the *synchronic* cityscape, which aims to reflect the transition of these ideas and the breaks with tradition as a reflection of function and history. Philosophically undetermined, it is a matter of taste to which design and artificiality, to which utopia one would like to give precedence.

New York City

MANHATTAN
Mechanical Contractors, Inc.

IMAGINE NY
giving voice to the people's visions

Hoy

RISE ABOVE

MANHATTAN FRUIT
EXCHANGE
24 HRS.
(212)989-2444 Fax(212)727-8124
PURVEYORS OF FRUITS & VEGETABLES TO THE FINER HOTEL/RESTAURANT

ENTERING
BURRITOVILLE

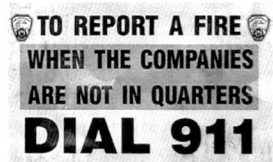
TO REPORT A FIRE
WHEN THE COMPANIES
ARE NOT IN QUARTERS
DIAL 911

AVAILABLE
NYC REALTY
201.227.9790

CITY STATIONERS CORP.
QUALITY • SERVICE • PRICE
SINCE 1946

MIDTOWN
ELECTRIC SUPPLY CORP
ELECTRICAL • LIGHTING • DATA
157 W. 18th St.
255-3388
LIGHTING SHOWROOM
LIGHTOLIER

Downtown
ALLiANCE

Famous FAMIGLIA
"NEW YORK'S
FAVORITE PIZZA"

Citi Habitats, Inc.
685-7300
LOFTS • BROWNSTONES • HI-RISE

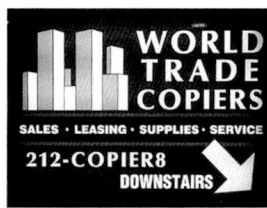
WORLD
TRADE
COPIERS
SALES • LEASING • SUPPLIES • SERVICE
212-COPIER8
DOWNSTAIRS

AVANTI

GRISTEDE'S
NEW YORK
MEGA STORES
100 YEARS

fig. 1: Collection of Icons and Logos before and after September 11

fig. 2: Famous Original and its Re-Enactment: Raising the Flag on Iwo Jima, Feb. 23 1945, Joe Rosenthal and Raising the Flag at Ground Zero, Sep. 11 2001, Thomas E. Franklin

genuine or canonical

The forcefulness of the event leads to the declamation of uniqueness. To examine this hypothesis it is possible to investigate the question of genuine image generation: "Nothing will be the same again!" Is the event already part of the *new world* or still part of the *old one*? Are the event and the subsequent reactions genuine, or transformations of what was before? Does the transformation conform to the allegedly different, the new?

In the reverse argument of reality the images of 9/11 correspond to the cultural production up to this date. The skyscraper, airplane and cinematography were all born at around the same time and have grown into the most significant attributes of a global civilization over the past hundred years. When poor visibility caused an American

bomber to fly into the Empire State Building in 1945 it was definitely not the first accident of this kind, and since the erection of skyscrapers it has been a requirement of their construction that they are able to withstand an aircraft impact. Aircraft hijacks have been part of the terrorist repertoire since the 1970s at the latest. Computer games and the film industry supply their audiences with countless variations on the destruction of buildings and cities. The images are not new; it seems the only factor determining their forcefulness is the dimension of their staging by the media.

The search for a genuine pictorial logic – by comparison with a historical classification and the cultural reception of global threat scenarios since Hiroshima and epically dramatic disasters like the sinking of the Titanic – is continued in the observation of the reactions. The picture of the three firefighters hoisting an American flag on the smoking ruins of the World Trade Center on September 11, 2001 quotes one of the most popular photographs of World War II in the United States, the photograph taken by Joe Rosenfeldt after the American conquest of the Pacific island of Iwo Jima on February 23, 1945 (**fig. 2**). In Iwo Jima the people performing this patriotic ritual are soldiers. Since 9/11 fire fighters and police officers have been promoted to the status of civilian soldiers and stylized as heroes in the daily battle against *Evil*. The picture has become an icon, it interacts with society and is replicated as a ritual, in the process losing its reference to the concrete event. What are the new images that, in light of the "symbolic challenge", go beyond the endlessly repeated picture of Osama bin Laden as a *kindly smiling man with a beard*?

symbol and status

The term 'symbol' is often used in situations in which it inadequately replaces the terms 'metaphor,' 'allegory,' 'sign' or 'icon'. When viewing or interpreting an object, a thing or an item as a *symbol* a misunderstanding often arises, namely that the attributes used are understood and used as genuine characteristics of the same object.

The phrases "symbol of global capitalism" and "phallic symbol" take us into the problems raised by this outlook. If the height of a building is sufficient for such symbols, the whole of Manhattan would consist of global-capitalist penises, from the Flatiron, the Woolworth Building and the Empire State Building, which were all the tallest buildings of their time, to the various

fig. 3: Lapsus 9/11

Trump Towers. This does not then provide an explanation of why the World Trade Center was chosen as a target. The crucial factor is not the general description (the largest global-capitalist penis of the United States is in Chicago), it is the specific that counts. The example of Babylonian symbolization suggests that there are relative, context-dependent definitions that would otherwise *mutatis mutandis* diametrically contradict the speaker's intentions.

For *symbolists* September 11 was the biggest event of all, a war of symbols: airplanes as symbols, skyscrapers as symbols and pictures as icons. The impression of the pictures gave rise to comments such as Baudrillard's "symbolic challenge", Lévi-Strauss's "loss of metaphysical intelligence" and Stockhausen's "artwork". Symbolizations serve the purpose of acquiring and instrumentalizing phenomena. They interpret and politicize in favor of subjective outlooks and ideas. Today it is hardly any longer possible to enumerate all the different symbolizations undergone by the World Trade Center from start to finish.

Opinions about the World Trade Center's aesthetic quality were controversial since its construction. Most New Yorkers and visitors preferred the Empire State Building to the plain architecture of the tall rectangular prisms. The disaster and the altered skyline have revised the aesthetic verdict. The formal stylization of the towers, two simple rectangles with a narrow line for the antenna, has substantially contributed to the creation of an icon. The towers are being replicated in all sorts of ways as souvenirs, devotional objects, tattoos and as window and front-garden decorations etc. Now that the concrete context has been removed, the icon becomes a cultural code in which faith and pride in the American nation come together with a quasi-religious fervor with projections of testing and salvation through virtues which one believes oneself to possess. It seems that buildings are being received for the first time in what is actually the human role of the martyr.

A further perspective of religious imagery is revealed if the iconoclasm of the Taliban regime, such as the destruction in March 2001 of the largest standing Buddha statues in the world in the Bamyan Valley were to be applied to the destruction of the twin towers of the WTC (assuming that the official version of Islamist terrorists from Osama bin Laden's organization were true).

Manhattan's nickname "Big Apple" forms the background to my comparison in **fig. 3**. When "Big Apple" was invented by some marketing strategists, dating back to the 1970s, it was conceived as an ironic comparison to Babylon and the alleged concentration of global sinfulness in New York. In *Lapsus 9/11* this image is prolonged through the iconography of the towers depicting a heterosexual couple, the promises of paradise, and the religiously based identity-formation and mythological self-determination of a society.

ground zero

Ground Zero: the point on the earth's surface directly above or below an exploding nuclear bomb, – the site of the former World Trade Center in New York City in the wake of the terrorist attacks of September 11, 2001, – figurative: a starting point or base for some activity
Oxford Dictionary

The world gathered in front of the television. New York gathered on the streets. Despite the event's global dimension and despite worldwide communication systems, the world remained but a spectator and only a small number were truly directly affected. While the international and national perspective soon focused on other subjects and conflicts, the regional perspective has remained glued to this plot of real estate. It is crucial for the understanding of the process to remember that this regional perspective attests to the reality of the events and their consequences for this place.

the foundations

The cleanup efforts were the preparation for building the future. Cleanup here meant recovering body parts and removing 1.6 million tons of rubble. What was left was a hole twenty meters deep with a huge concrete wall from which all the remains of what was before were scraped out. The discrepancy between the site's apparent neutrality and its historical significance is indescribable. An empty space middle in the city. Both the towers and the ruins have disappeared. The scene already resembles a building site and it will remain this way for the next few years.

Parallel to the preparation of the foundations the search for the basis of future plans is continuing. The early speculations and ambitions fell silent, as was to be expected, since no easy answer was to be found to the complexity of the situation. The big questions were put on the back-burner while the small issues were addressed. The process continued to develop as large numbers of the public contributed and got organized. On the basis of diverse personal initiatives a way was sought for all those involved to reach a consensus. The public process turned the question into the answer. The reaction of the community replaced the reaction on behalf of the community. The question was not 'what?', it was 'how?' However, this turned the process itself into an object of discussion.

The discussions of the past months show that one subject has occupied people's thoughts and feelings more than any other: it is the question about the structures of power, influence and co-determination in this process. There have been different answers to this question at different times. Only when the result is truly hard-and-fast we will be able to see who had what share in it. But even then the result should not be equated with the process.

the site

The plot on which the World Trade Center once stood is in downtown Manhattan, in the Financial District, near Wall Street, and next to the World Financial Center, between West Street, Vesey Street, Church Street, and Liberty Street. Between the plot and the WFC is the West Side Highway, which runs southbound into Brooklyn Battery Tunnel, a main artery between Manhattan and Brooklyn. St. Paul's church and churchyard are to the east.

The World Trade Center possessed its own zip code: *New York 10047/48*. The plot is an irregular trapezoid, almost square, and is six and a half hectares in area. The land is the property of the *Port Authority of New York & New Jersey* (PANYNJ), a bi-state dock and transportation body that leased all of the WTC buildings for 99 years to the Larry Silverstein Consortium in July 2001.

The WTC was planned as a "super block" over more than twelve existing blocks, thereby interrupting the historical street pattern. Until September 11 the infrastructure consisted of a terminus for *PATH* trains (Port Authority Trans Hudson), three subway stations, ten transformers of Consolidated Edison in *7 WTC* and one 100m antenna on the North Tower for Verizon.

the situation

14 % of tax income and a quarter of the economic capacity of New York City come from the financial services sector. Of the 370,000 jobs in Lower Manhattan, 49 % are in this sector, which generates 77 % of the turnover in Lower Manhattan. Lower Manhattan is the third-largest economic center in the United States, after Midtown Manhattan and Chicago. Of the 3.7 million jobs in NYC, 10 % were in Lower Manhattan. 1,250 companies operated in the WTC's seven buildings. After 9/11, 100,000 jobs were relocated to Midtown or to other areas outside of the city.

2.3 million square meters of office space, 30 % of Lower Manhattan, were destroyed or rendered unusable, of which one million square meters were in the destroyed WTC complex, 300,000 square meters were severely damaged and one million square meters could soon be used again after swift refurbishments. Of the big companies like American Express, Morgan Stanley and Goldman Sachs, many were to return with a majority of their employees. However, the trend of decentralization is gradually asserting itself in business management, so that certain resources remained or were newly installed in different locations.

The economic damage of the 9/11 attacks is currently estimated to be around 83 billion dollars. That corresponds to almost a fifth (19 %) of the economic capacity of New York City (440 billion dollars). After subtracting insurance payouts and the state grants, the remaining loss is relatively low at 16 billion dollars. Since that time around 100,000 jobs have been lost in the city. It is believed that this figure will drop to 57,000 fewer jobs by the end of 2003. Since mid-September unemployment has risen from 5 % to 7.5 %.

Great losses were suffered by the tourist industry (25,000 jobs), retail (a 14 % decline), the real-estate market (rents in Lower Manhattan fell by 13 %) and smaller service providers (approximately 1,000 bankruptcies). Passenger flights have dropped by 20 %.

The great competitor for NYC as a location is nearby Jersey City on the other side of the Hudson River. In recent years large businesses have been increasingly locating here, which can be seen very clearly by the fast growing skyline. For that reason New York is at pains to develop, as quickly as possible, areas in the five city boroughs into attractive economic locations which could deliver the right infrastructure and cheaper property prices.

The disaster of the 9/11 attacks has acted as a catalyst to accelerate almost all the trends towards economic restructuring: the recession, the fall of share prices after the burst dot-com bubble, the decline in the labor market as well as the decentralization in company location policy and the resulting concepts for town planning.

from ground zero to fresh kills

Fresh Kills (from the Middle Dutch word kille, meaning "riverbed" or "water channel") is a stream and freshwater estuary in the western portion of the New York City borough of Staten Island. It is the site of the Fresh Kills Landfill, formerly New York City's principal landfill. http://en.wikipedia.org

By the end of May 2002 the recovery and cleanup work was complete and 1.6 million tons of rubble and ruins had been removed (200,000 tons of steel from the towers). This was half a year ahead of schedule. Volunteers from all over the country came to help with the cleanup operation. Work continued day and night. The volunteers were given room and board by yet more voluntary helpers.

Floodlights provided not just the necessary illumination but also an at times ethereal mood over the pit, which is still sealed off by police. To make sure as little harmful dust as possible was thrown up during transport the streets as well as the incoming and departing lorries were kept moist with water.

While the toxic dust deposits on the façades and in the streets have dissipated as a result of wind erosion, the pollution of private homes by dust from the WTC building materials (which contained asbestos and heavy metals) continues to be a problem: as a result of improper removal, properly cleaned areas were once again contaminated. The risks for people's health are incalculable. In May the Environmental Protection Agency announced it would take on the task of cleaning up private homes. This delayed measure is likely to prove critical for the health of some inhabitants, leading to the filing of a class-action lawsuit against Washington.

In May some of the surrounding buildings still displayed damage from the collapse of the twin towers. Of the eleven subway stations closed, eight started operating again in December. A visitor platform was installed, giving tourists a view for which they have to pay. The proceeds go into a special fund for the bereaved.

The rubble of the seven buildings was driven by lorry to the nearby Hudson River, where it was transferred to ships and then taken to the re-opened *Fresh Kills Landfill*. Some of the steel construction was sent to a *salvage yard* in Newark for detailed examination of the causes of the collapse.

The Fresh Kills Landfill is thought to be the largest manmade structure and, like the Great Wall of China, is said to be visible from space. A huge open-air laboratory has been created there in which the waste deliveries are searched for human remains, objects of value and data carriers. A first call for the relatives of victims to provide DNA-containing personal effects was followed by a second in March 2002, since the material provided was not sufficient to run a DNA analysis which could identify the victims. Of the 2825 who died, the remains of somewhat more than a third have been identified to date.

Consideration about what to do with the 19,132 bones and other non-identifiable remains is pending. It is probable that they will be buried in a grave of the unknown victims of 9/11 until a later date when better analysis techniques are available. Until then they are being kept in thirty refrigerated containers on 30th Street.

Several funds were set up for the victims of the 9/11 attacks, such as for relatives of the firefighters, police officers and employees who died in the buildings as well as for the schooling of the children of those who died, for the inhabitants of Lower Manhattan, for small businesses, and also for artists and designers.

the process

The rebuilding of Lower Manhattan is now seen as the biggest project in the United States and will remain thus for the next few years. This project is accompanied by equally great public interest. The public demand that this process be comprehensive and open to all those affected and involved and that it be made into the principle of a joint search for the future.

Producing a master plan with so many different implications is no easy task. It is a time-consuming process, not least because in the centers of the largest economic nations major projects have to go through a long and complicated approval procedure at all levels.

After September 11 several hundred groups and initiatives got together to address direct tasks and problems and to deal with upcoming questions. Some of them only had limited life-spans, while others have expanded their goals to be involved in future planning and design. Assuming forty of these groups to be still active and every one of them to have been founded by members from around 30 already extant institutions and organizations (e.g. NYNV: 22; NYC Partnership: 40; Civic Alliance: 100), it would appear that there are 1200 groups involved in the rebuilding of Lower Manhattan. This calculation illustrates the dimensions of the process. Absolute numbers are hard to give because many people are active in several groups concurrently, and universities are acting as providers of scientific resources and main sponsors for several initiatives.

The following list gives people, groups and institutions in direct connection with the discussions about the rebuilding of Lower Manhattan, nearly half of them were formed after 9/11:

September's Mission – Rebuilding with a Spotlight on the Poor, SPOT – Wallstreetrising – Widows and Families 911 – Rebuild Downtown Our Town, R.DoT – Regional Planning Association, RPA – Families of September 11 – Give Your Voice WTC – New York State Governor Pataki – Ground Zero Task Force – Labor Community Advocacy Network – Larry Silverstein Consortium – Lower Manhattan Development Corporation, LMDC – Civic Alliance to Rebuild Lower Manhattan – NYC Partnership – New York New Visions, NYNV – Community Boards No. 1, 2, 3 – Downtown Alliance – Municipal Art Society, MAS – NYC Rebuild – City Council's Select Committee on Lower Manhattan Redevelopment – City Planning Commission – Empire State Transportation Alliance – Mayor Bloomberg – Mass Transportation Authority, MTA – Office of Regional and Community Affairs of the Federal Reserve Bank of New York, ORCA – Port Authority New York New Jersey, PANYNJ – Real Estate Board of New York

distributions of power

Lower Manhattan Development Corporation

The LMDC is a subsidiary of the Empire State Development Corporation New York, ESDC. It is subject to the instructions of the governor. The state corporation was established last autumn by Governor Pataki and Mayor Giuliani to take over responsibility for the development and reconstruction of the World Trade Center and Lower Manhattan. Seven members of the commission were appointed by Pataki, four by Giuliani. They have all come from the higher echelons of *Big Business* and have the corresponding connections to politicians. Since Mayor Bloomberg had not had any say in the planning the commission was expanded by three further members appointed by him in March.

The LMDC appointed Alexander Garvin as director of planning, design and development in March. Furthermore several working groups were formed that will address the various subject areas. The complicated structure of the commission has begun to resemble that of an administrative authority.

Amongst its most important tasks are supervision, contact with the public, co-ordination with the city, the state and with Washington, as well as the distribution of the 20 billion dollars from Washington. The LMDC is considered the crucial interface between the institutions, the decision-makers involved and the public.

Port Authority of New York & New Jersey

The PANYNJ is the owner of the site and until 2001 it also owned and operated the World Trade Center. It only leased it to Larry Silverstein for 99 years at the end of July 2001.

The Port Authority is an organization that belongs in equal parts to the state of New York and the state of New Jersey. It is the only bi-state organization in the United States. It owns the three major airports John F. Kennedy, La Guardia and Newark as well as all the bridges and tunnels that connect the islands of New York as well as New York with New Jersey. It also operates two subway lines, the PATH trains (Port Authority Trans Hudson), which run below the Hudson River between Jersey City and Manhattan. On the site of the WTC is one of the four hubs of the PATH system, which is used by 50,000 commuters on their way to work downtown every day.

The Port Authority, in its capacity as owner, is one of the decisive figures in the question about the future of Ground Zero.

Larry Silverstein Consortium

It was only at the end of July 2001 that Larry Silverstein signed a 99-year lease on the six buildings of the World Trade Center from the Port Authority, six weeks before the September 11 attack.

Larry Silverstein had already taken a lease on the building known as 7 WTC, located north of the plaza, also Port Authority property, as early as the 1980s. It collapsed on 9/11 at around 6pm local time as a result of the damage caused by the collapse of the North Tower. Since its destruction, Silverstein has wanted to have the building reconstructed on the same groundplan. After vehement protests by the public against his plans to construct a building with the same dimensions as its predecessor, which would have prevented the reintroduction of the grid-pattern, namely through the extension of Greenwich Street, he declared himself willing to limit the new building to one side of the street and forgo 20 % of office space. The construction work for a new 7 WTC began in May.

There are several reasons why Silverstein was given a relatively free hand in developing this piece of real estate: different contractual obligations, the geographical distance, acknowledgement of his company's turnover as well as the need to replace the ten transformers of ConEdison, which would consolidate Lower Manhattan's electricity supply. With regard to the site of the WTC his input potential is severely limited. There are four reasons for this: the argument about the insurance premium, the complex ownership and interest situation, dependence on economic developments, and the time factor.

The Silverstein Consortium is currently involved in an absurd legal battle with the insurance companies about the amount of the insurance payout. Silverstein claims there were two separate events, two aircraft, two attacks. The insurance company claims it was one terrorist attack with two airplanes. Depending on how the federal judges decide, Silverstein would receive either 3.5 billion dollars or 7 billion dollars. The outcome of this trial is an explosive issue, for if the court were to go along with the version that there were two separate events, it is likely there would be large-scale political implications. At the moment several factors suggest the two parties will settle out of court.

After initial reactions that demanded the World Trade Center be rebuilt true to the original, Silverstein went public with his concept of four identical buildings half the height of the twin towers. For many it was a sign that once again the decision-making power was in the hands of individual powerful people.

Meanwhile the actual situation is different, because as the leaseholder Silverstein is bound to his contractual obligations toward the Port Authority. The state corporation is subordinate to the governors of the states of New York and New Jersey. The public, the government and private businesses all have an interest. In addition the growing organization of opinion and interest groups has established itself as an equal dialogue partner for the future of Lower Manhattan and the site of the WTC.

Since the effects of September 11 have affected the functions of the city so comprehensively, Silverstein, like everyone else, is dependent on the city's revitalization. Washington has agreed to donate 20 billion dollars for the development program. Silverstein can only hope to make a profitable turnover from renting out his new WTC if business activity improves. It would be unwise of him not to behave with due co-operation.

New York State Governor George E. Pataki

Governor Pataki is considered to be one of the most influential persons involved in planning the WTC site (**fig. 11**, p. 46/47). Of the 14 board members of the LMDC he has appointed seven, including the chairman John C. Whitehead and the president and executive director Louis Tomson. The LMDC is a division of the ESDC, which is chaired by Charles Gargano, a close colleague and confidant of Pataki. In addition Governor Pataki controls the Port Authority together with the newly elected Governor McGreedy of New Jersey, who has not yet made his mark. Pataki has appointed six of the twelve board members; furthermore the post of vice president is held by his close colleague Charles A. Gargano.

Pataki is already campaigning for the upcoming elections for the office of governor of New York in November. His potential Democratic opponent Andrew Cuomo recently maintained with great media effect that the development of Ground Zero was proceeding too slowly. His success at the election will depend on the public perception of his performance in this process.

NYC Mayor Mike Bloomberg

In December Bloomberg was elected mayor of New York, succeeding Rudolph Giuliani. Giuliani had established himself as the man of *Zero Tolerance* regarding public security and as a comforting and stable crisis manager after the September 11 attacks.

Bloomberg, who does not see himself as a politician, but as a manager, faces the difficult challenge of getting a grip on economic reconstruction, negative budget balance sheets and unemployment. His role in the rebuilding of the World Trade Center is a more of an symbolic one, since he does not have many means of influence.

Community Boards

Community Boards are independent organizations of inhabitants of locally limited areas. Since the grassroots/civil rights movements of the 1960s their significance and their political influence have grown substantially. They work in close co-operation with local political institutions. No project can be implemented without prior presentation to, discussion with and approval by the "Community".

There are currently 20,000 people living in Lower Manhattan. The WTC site lies on the boundary between CB#1 and #2.

public process

The *public process* is to be conceived of as a construct of an conceptual whole composed of different public, private, social and civil initiatives.

The public process reveals an image of the general public's mood on the one hand and on the other it is capable of generating ideas, energies and creativity that go beyond the institutional and administrative resources. It is a corrective entity in the decision-making and idea-finding process. The principle of public participation is also a fundamental principle of applied democracy.

The public process takes place at different levels: it becomes visible in the unorganized, uncontrolled expressions of opinion that can be seen on spontaneous memorials, candlelight processions, shrines and remembrance plaques. In surveys, workshops and public events attempts are made to get a measurable picture of public opinion based on sociological and statistical structures.

Thirdly, the self-organization of civil society into private and public groups and interest groups can be observed. In order to take on social, economic or political responsibility it is crucial that these groups can call on existing and functioning communication structures and successful lobbying. The internet, as a multiplier in global network and information exchange, plays a big role in the *open source* movement of public processes.

At the start of all public participation are the many spontaneous memorials dotted all over the city, some of which are still being refurbished and maintained. The "Missing" posters have developed into an art form of their own (**img. 2-7, p. 33**).

Next, there are the many suggestions, ideas and designs that reached the different institutions and initiatives in their thousands and whose quantity goes beyond existing capacities, which is why there are several initiatives for the purpose of organizing these contributions.

The first initiative of public participation was the exhibition *Here is New York. A Democracy of Photographs*, which opened in early October. It was the initiator's aim to use the archiving of photographic material to make the experiences of every individual accessible to the general public and to create a collective pool of photographic memories. The distinction between professional and amateur photographs was deliberately avoided. The photographs that were handed in were digitalized and archived. Some of them were exhibited in the gallery space. Visitors could buy them as A3 prints. The profits of $25 per print went to an initiative for the children of those who died. Since its opening in October the onrush of visitors has hardly diminished. *Here is New York* has since been continued in other cities around the world. In August an excerpt from the pictures was also shown at the Martin-Gropius-Bau in Berlin.

The coalition known as NewYorkNewVisions came together just a few days after September 11 in order to examine joint strategies for New York, Manhattan, Ground Zero and the overall process of thinking and planning. One tenet is the commitment to work for a comprehensive, public process on the basis of public acceptance. Subjects such as transport, infrastructure, culture, town planning and memorial processes are addressed in seven working groups.

As early as November the *Memorial Process* working group held discussions in which those affected and the representatives of different interest groups commented on the possibilities of commemoration and the creation of a cenotaph or memorial (victims' family members, recovery workers, inhabitants, real estate owners, businesspeople, leading businesses etc.).

The *Temporary Memorials* working group has contributed a lot to moving the process itself more firmly into the horizon of the debate on planning and commemoration, thereby introducing the component of time against the claim of permanence. Temporary Memorials has published a series of periodically appearing maps that depict how the situation at Ground Zero, the condition of the surrounding buildings and the mourning and memorial walls have changed.

In December NYNV produced a report containing principles for the rebuilding of Lower Manhattan. This pamphlet was welcomed as the first significant piece of city planning after the introduction of the grid pattern in 1811. The principles developed here were adopted almost unchanged into the official design presented by the Lower Manhattan Development Corporation in April.

On November 15 the New York City Partnership, a spontaneous union of leading corporate consultants (McKinsey, KPMG etc.), presented its first report on the economic consequences of September 11 for New York's economy. It is a study written and conducted on the partnership's own initiative and interest and provides precise information about the state of the affected industries and instructions about how a fast recovery can be achieved.

Dissatisfied with the state of the discussion surrounding the rebuilding of the WTC site, the New York gallery owner Max Protetch conceived the idea for the exhibition *A New World Trade Center*. In January he opened the controversial, but yet successful exhibition with 35 ambitious designs and ideas by internationally famous architects for a new World Trade Center. Criticism focused on the attitude of artistically trivializing the situation through the presumptuous self-confidence of the designing individual.

In January Exit Art opened its exhibition *Reactions*. Exit Art received around 10,000 international contributions following an advertisement asking what September 11 had meant to people and how it had changed their lives or perspectives. The responses on sheets of paper in US letter format are all exhibited in the gallery.

The *Civic Alliance to Rebuild Downtown New York* put on the first big public hearing on February 7. Approx. 600 people attended the Alliance's *Listening to the City* event, where they were able to voice their worries, concerns, ideas and desires about the process and the upcoming tasks facing those responsible in private and governmental institutions.

The *Civic Alliance* considers itself a kind of umbrella organization for the many private and public planning ambitions. More than 100 business associations, citizens' groups, environmental and planning groups have come together here to formulate a common vision for the future of Ground Zero and Lower Manhattan. It works closely with the LMDC, the Port Authority and the New York City Planning Commission. The Regional Planning Association, RPA, and a group of academic partners such as New York University, New School University and Pratt Institute PICCED are making personnel and other resources available. The Civic Alliance has just as large and complex a structure of working groups and employees as the LMDC. It is often the case that the same people are represented in both organizations. This duplication also occurs in the Civic Alliance and its founding organizations, such as NewYorkNewVisions.

The light installation opened for 31 days on March 11, *Tribute in Light* (originally *Towers of Light*), is also a project implemented on private initiative and through the commitment and support of non-governmental organizations. A few days after September 11 two similar suggestions were made independently of each other about a light sculpture of two rays of light to commemorate the twin towers of the WTC. Under the agency of the Municipal Art Society the artists and architects came together in a single team. The idea quickly gained general recognition and by the time it was implemented it had become common knowledge. "It's nice! The lights are cool!" was the general reaction to the towers of light that projected kilometers into the sky for the first time on March 11. While acknowledging the lights' temporary character, many said it was unfortunate that they had to watch the twin towers disappear a second time.

In March discussion turned to fencing in the area during the foundation works and the reconstruction of the subway tunnels and stations. After the executive director of the Port Authority suggested a 10-meter-high wooden barrier to protect the public from seeing the building site, he was hit with a wave of protest so that he was forced to confront a different option. In a *non-public* meeting with different participants from private planning initiatives, including NYNV, a fence was designed that did not deny the location's significance to the people; it was designed as a permeable envelope that accommodates the different needs of commemoration and commiseration.

In April the *Municipal Art Society*, together with New York University, New School University and the Pratt Institute Center for Community and Environmental Development, held its workshop series *Imagine New York*. More than a hundred seminars were held in all of New York's boroughs as well as in New Jersey and Connecticut. The goal was to capture the mood of the general public in order to create a foundation for plans accepted by everyone. Three questions needed to be answered: "What have we lost and how have we changed? What should the future look like? What superordinate themes can be derived from this?" (**fig. 13**, p. 50/51)

More than 2,000 people participated. The enormous wealth of data was sorted, filtered and statistically evaluated. The results were presented in July. They portray a surprisingly consistent consensus of opinion, since the same superordinate principles are reflected in the different neighborhoods.

In July the Lower Manhattan Development Corporation and the Civic Alliance arranged the largest public citizens' meeting about the future of the WTC site: *Listening to the City II*. More than 5,000 participants were present and discussed not only their ideas but also concepts by Beyer, Blinder & Belle, which had been published a few days earlier. The event was supported with a system of electronic data-registering by *America Speaks*, so that the voting results could be determined immediately.

principles newyorknewvisions

1. An Open Memorial Process
Organize a formal, transparent, and open process to determine the nature and location of memorials. Ultimately, memorials should be integral to the redevelopment of the area. Prepare for a

lengthy and comprehensive memorial effort. Establish appropriate temporary memorials during the intervening period.

2. A Flexible Mixed-Use Future for Lower Manhattan

Intensify and encourage increased diversity of uses. Capitalize on the cultural, historic, and geographic assets of the district as generators of growth. Develop a true 24-hour community within a pedestrian realm. Promote complementary adjacencies to improve security, protect real estate values and ensure economic vitality.

3. A More Connected Downtown

Focus on improving accessibility by mass transit –it is the single most important investment in the future health of Lower Manhattan. Magnify public and economic benefits of investment by linking existing and new transportation centers and integrating them with pedestrian flows and public spaces. Simply replacing the transit capabilities lost on September 11 will not create the full potential for Lower Manhattan in the 21st century. Consider creating a 'Grand Central Station' for downtown.

4. A Renewed Relationship of Lower Manhattan and the Region

Implement a balanced growth strategy that reflects the reciprocal relationship of Lower Manhattan and the region. Coordinate decisions about the restructuring of the World Trade Center site with development in the rest of Manhattan, the other city boroughs, and key communities in Long Island, Westchester and New Jersey.

5. Design Excellence and Sustainability for New York City

Demand design excellence with an emphasis on sustainability to create long-lasting economic and social value. Create the highest quality urban design and architecture. Require decreased life-cycle costs and energy use. Promote long-term flexibility. Provide robust and redundant energy, security and telecommunications systems.

6. An Effective and Inclusive Planning Process

Create a comprehensive plan for Lower Manhattan with long and short term strategies. Accomplish the plan through a participatory process involving government, private sector, and the public. Balance urgency with informed decisions. Reorganize the building review process to expedite priority projects. Adopt a model building code to address changes in technology and performance.

7. Immediate Action

Create and implement a plan for temporary memorials, integrated with viewing places that address visitor and resident needs. Address short-term transportation, amenity, and small-business needs of the district. Define the character of a secure and open public realm, and begin its implementation as utilities are put back into place.

(NYNV Report Feb. 2002)

structures

Right from the start the question of power was a central subject of every discussion. It is telling that to this day no definitive answer is possible. Even though tendencies that have become consolidated over the course of the observation can be determined, the process remains open toward changing opinion patterns and the influence of the media and politicians. One thing that can be seen is that certain chronological events attracted the attention and public perception with regard to the question of the distribution of power:

In September many people thought that Larry Silverstein was the owner and that he will rebuild the towers just as they were.

In October the Bush administration in Washington promised to support the rebuilding of New York with 20 billion dollars.

In November it seemed as if the LMDC, founded by the state and city of New York, would control the rebuilding process.

In December Mayor Giuliani took the side of the victims' families, who demanded that the entire area be dedicated as a cemetery.

In January Mike Bloomberg became Mayor Giuliani's successor.

In February the Civic Alliance held its first major conference with 600 participants, and NewYorkNewVisions and NYC Partnership published their final reports.

In March the LMDC commission was expanded so that New York City and New York State would have the same number of posts. LMDC published its reconstruction guidelines.

In April LMCD and the Port Authority agreed a distribution of tasks and called for designs to be submitted. The Port Authority made it clear that it would have the say about the future of the site.

These changes are thus only apparent changes, and yet they are much more than just nominal. In every phase a new layer is placed on the framework of responsibilities. Thus it remains to be seen, for example, what happens if the monument were to become a formal national memorial and Washington became involved as the responsible owner.

the phases

The first phase is characterized on the one hand by the event's consequences and their removal, as well as an incipient discourse on the other. Before new plans could be made an intensive discussion took place in New York about the value of different concepts which could portray contemporary principles in city development. The results of the public co-operation were adopted into the principles of the official and business authorities. These principles represent a minimal consensus that leaves open many controversial positions for further discussions.

The second phase is marked by the end of the recovery and clearance works. In May 2002 construction for the rebuilding of 7 WTC and the stations and tunnels of the subway system and PATH trains was begun.

In addition the Port Authority and the LMDC started the official invitation for city planning concepts for the WTC. In a competition limited to New York with 13 participants, Beyer Blinder Belle Architects & Planners LLP was chosen to develop the first master-plan for the site.

The competition was part of a schedule the Port Authority had created at the end of April. The second phase marked the appearance of the institutions and administrative authorities as active participants. The Port Authority's schedule emphasizes its dominant role in the planning process, which has caused it to be criticized for thwarting the previous efforts and co-operation of many participants.

The process entered a further phase in July 2002. The first concepts of the master plan by Beyer Blinder Belle were presented and, as a result of vehement criticism at a public congress with 5,000 participants, promptly scrapped. In the future it is likely that the task distribution will be shaped to a greater extent by the institutions' actions and the public's reaction than by a joint course of action.

wtc and lower manhattan

In order to face up to the many uncertainties that have emerged in looking at this problem, it is first necessary to distinguish between two spatial zones, a distinction that is frequently neglected: Lower Manhattan and the site of the World Trade Center. On the one hand a district, on the other a complex of buildings whose dominance reaches far beyond this district. The future lies in mutual dependence. The Center needs the surrounding area, the surrounding area needs the Center. Although the WTC was in a sense a district in its own right, its infrastructure also supplied Lower Manhattan (with transportation, news technology, energy etc.) and vice versa (**fig. 4**, p. 37).

As a result of the interplay, and connected by the common cause, many participants think of both tasks at the same time and favour an holistic concept over possible individual solutions.

However, the structures of responsibility for the one area and the other area differ too much for that.

The future of the WTC is dependent on consensus between four parties: the Port Authority as the freeholder, the leaseholder Larry Silverstein, the Lower Manhattan Development Corporation and the public (**fig. 5**, p. 36). The state of New York and Governor Pataki are behind the Port Authority (PA) and LMDC. This faction is undoubtedly the most powerful. Nevertheless there are significant uncertainties between these two regarding their competencies. In April it was agreed that the Port Authority would strengthen the responsibilities for the planning of a new WTC, while the LMDC would take over the co-ordination of the process for Lower Manhattan, the public participation, as well as the development of a time frame for constituting a memorial. Contrary to the general assumption that the decisions are being made by the real-estate developer Larry Silverstein, the Port Authority will be responsible for awarding planning contracts.

The scale on which the public process will incorporate itself into the design ideas and the framework is an interesting question that cannot, however, be predicted exactly. Before the final decision is made, enough time will pass for doubt and reconsideration. The success of the public process will have to be measured by the degree of participation in both projects, the site of the WTC and the plans for Lower Manhattan (**fig. 6**, p. 38/39).

A closer qualitative examination reveals the critical relationship of the power distribution: the graphic (**fig. 10**, p. 44/45) is developed by using the triangle form of hierarchical structures. At the top is the WTC site with the question of future use. The right-hand sector shows the concentration of the public process in the lower part of the triangle. The left-hand sector shows the concentration of governmental influence in the upper area. Larry Silverstein is part of the non-governmental area, but not part of the public process. The politics/economy and media/public opinion poles as abstract entities form a further force field.

By mirroring the left-hand area the result is a triangle standing on its apex, which represents the polarized distribution of influencing powers between the governmental and the public side. A reduced Scheme of **fig. 10** can be used to explore this fundamental relationship. Where and how do the triangles meet? Can a general difference between the political systems of the United States and the countries of Europe be formulated in this way?

critique

Although the attempt to depict the relationships in this process remains unsatisfactory, some trends can still be determined: this is about the fundamental differences in the structures of the community. The distribution of social tasks in the United States gives individual responsibility a greater input than European systems do. It is not uncommon for decision-making structures to be structured not top down, but bottom up.

This aspect of the US political system can be illustrated by an example from New York's city planning: the concept of a regular grid pattern as the framework of non-restrictive, equal and unlimited development. The setting of a minimum, socially *good* and comprehensive consensus solution and the obligation on individuals to do their part correspond to the observations I have made in this process.

By means of this discussion it would be possible to move on to the applicability and comparability for local planning processes in Germany. To what extent could the New York process be a role model and how far-reaching is the exceptional nature of the situation in which it is taking place? There is no easy answer to this. The processes hitherto have been motivated by special conditions. 9/11 thrust a city into a kind of state of war: after the physical destruction and the general economic aftershock all citizens were affected. The collective consciousness was fully focused on repair. Knowledge of the enormous financial pressure accelerated the public initiatives to act faster than the institutional side of the government and business in their search for viable solutions. The uncontrolled, spontaneous involvement of the people had a structural head start here, which it lost again over time.

The critique on the role of the public process is shaped by the discussion at different levels. The *international* critics complain about the lack of a debate on the place the event holds in global politics and the lack of a self-critical search for causes, such as solving the paradox of the re-building in Lower Manhattan and Afghanistan. Furthermore the unilateral isolation and the ex-clusion of international participation has created the impression that America considered itself sufficient unto itself in this respect.

My observations and experiences show that the process does not exclude anyone; there is, how-ever, no concept by which the integration of the global public could be organized. I would ex-clude this general perspective in this discussion and make a case for a differentiated look at in-dividual processes. Just as New York and Wa-shington are centers with different dispositions, there are also different processes that are linked. Looking at basic processes produces individual results that can also be discussed independently. The justification of the *regional* perspective lies in the real, material involvement and the avo-idance of rushed interpretations in highly critical political associations. For the above-mentioned reasons I think limiting the discussion solely to the quality of the regional process is justified.

The collaboration of all those affected is seen as a continuation of the *spirit of helpfulness and community* that existed in the days after Sep-tember 11. This is consensus, it is politics, but it is definitely also piety. Differences in opinion, cheap power struggles and political maneuvers must, it is felt, not impede the cohesion and uni-on that seem appropriate in view of the victims, the terror and the consequences. However, since so much has stayed the same, this commitment often shrinks to a thin cover that now only pre-tends to maintain the appearance.

Now there are at least two readings critics use in order to question the role of the public in this process: the one assumes therapy, the other a form of political theatre. The former opinion holds that the public participation and commise-ration is a form of talk therapy that does not have any serious goal-oriented aims. It is merely an attempt to cope with the post-traumatic impact. The others see the process as a puppet theatre in which the voluntary actors are controlled by the interests of the powerful, while the appearan-ce of political and moral propriety in terms of their instrumentalization has to be maintained. Finally there is a third, socio-philosophical dis-cussion that examines the influence and interest of the "public process" in searching for and de-termining the "common good" from a historical-critical perspective.

The existence of the object is justified by the existence of its criticism. The process, the struc-ture of searches for content, have themselves become objects of a dispute regarding content and have thereby replaced the discussion of con-crete questions of design regarding the site and the rebuilding.

In view of the productive work, the intelligence of the initiatives and my own experience on the spot I judge the accusation of therapy to be un-founded. Of course this is also about working through the psychological processes of pain, mourning, helplessness, trauma, loss, existenti-al threats and altered perceptions. However, the constructive nature of the process is created by the need to get out of the recession and to get rid of unemployment.

Moving on from the theory of therapy, with regard to a common instrument called *Public-Private-Partnership*, the critique would lead to a theory of the political theatre, which is staged to

veil the the marginal nature of the public and the extensive power of the economic influence. The influence of business interests can be demonstrated as follows:
– The commission of the Lower Manhattan Development Corporation is full of people who are from the executive floors of big businesses and have close ties to politicians. Only one member works in local government.
– Although the Port Authority is a governmental organization, economically it is completely independent of the state and for that reason it too responds fully in accordance with market-economic principles.
– For Larry Silverstein this is definitely about a lot of money.

In November elections for the office of governor of the state of New York will take place. The re-election of the Republican Pataki very much depends on how voters perceive the success of his work on the rebuilding process. His potential Democratic opponent Andrew M. Cuomo is trying to discredit Pataki's role exactly in this regard for his election campaign: he has accused Pataki of lacking leadership in this process and has complained that everything is moving forward too slowly.

The slow nature of the progress is the result of its complicated structures and of the involvement of the many different groups. Given that Cuomo criticizes this, he is reducing the chances of a comprehensive public process, which seems to contradict his political instinct as a Democrat and, as a pure election campaign maneuver, negates the work done so far. Even though the accusation is double-edged, Pataki and his two leading institutions have reacted and increased the tempo. It remains to be seen whether this too is just a political maneuver to take the wind out of his political opponent's sails.

In April the LMDC and Port Authority presented a schedule for the development of the World Trace Center site whose unexpected density is amazing:
– In May Beyer, Blinder and Belle was chosen from fifteen primarily New York-based architectural offices who participated in a competition announced at short notice.
– The intention is for them to present their first results for a master-plan by July 2002; a firm schedule for a competition for the memorial is also to be in place by then.
– By September 2002 the decision on the final design will be made.
– The plan is for work to commence in December.

The first competition about the future of Ground Zero was held on the quiet. The Port Authority considers itself responsible for the decision about a master-plan for the site of the World Trade Center and did not involve a jury, nor invite entries to an international competition. This approach generated surprisingly little public criticism.

the desert

It is appropriate at this point to note the experimental character of the American past and its cultural and social development. The *desert* as an aesthetic category corresponds to the idea of freedom to prove oneself in the lawlessness of a particular present and to cross boundaries on allegedly neutral ground. The desert has always been a place of temptation and introspection. The Western as genre, the detonation of nuclear devices in Nevada, and the invention of the road movie: ever since the Biblical accounts, genesis and catharsis have taken place in the remoteness of deserts.

When I came to New York I was looking for a personal design conception. My presence and research on location showed me that this kind of subjective opinion was still inappropriate at the time. A form of collective designing had taken on this task in New York. The democratic consensus following the events of the September 11 seemed to support the nature of architecture as a social medium. I tried to support this work through my participation in the working groups.

It would have been a valuable task, with an experimental character, to continue this public design process in this intensity and on this scale. It would have been a *unique* response to the "unprecedented event". The transition from phase 1 to phase 2 shows that the quality of the public process also redounds to its disadvantage because the openness and comprehensive participation in the conflict leads to a lack of direction. At this stage the work that had been begun was interrupted and continued in the conventional manner, i.e. authorities delegated their competencies. Could the functional schema of public consensus not have served as a design template on which the public process continued to act as a planner in order thereby to continue the search for the "essential nature of the task"?

With reference to the discussed diagrams, a situation can be created in which the decisions for the future of the WTC site will be made at a higher level, with the public excluded (**fig. 12**, p. 48/49). Right from the start the question of power was a central subject of every discussion and people hoped this exclusion would not take place; in other words, that New York would not go back to "business as usual". There is a wall separating the public from the procedure and replacing its action by its reaction.

Following the presentation of these critical factors, the impression of the significance of the *public process* disappears. It is not, however, the actual distribution of power but the thematic substance, the qualitative influence, that should be decisive when making a judgement: the work on a collective commemoration of 9/11, the community of voluntary workers and the formulation of a social consensus make up the precondition for further processes affecting the future of Ground Zero.

The question remains open whether the altered role the public now has will discredit the assessment of its previous significance and whether the response of the cultural reaction in the historical and symbolic context turns out differently from what we would have liked to assume.

With reference to Heidegger's phenomenology, an aesthetic conceptualization of the process and the role of the public could be developed: the artwork as concretion of meaning condenses the interconnected associations of existence. If a place is torn out of the conception of its conventionalized appearance with such violence as the towers and the plaza of the World Trade Center were, then it takes some cultural effort to anchor it again in society and overcome the emptiness.

The architect Rem Koolhaas said in October 2001 that it was too early for architects to present their designs, one would have to "wait until a new cultural balance had developed". This condition has now been fulfilled. The intensive public process has contributed to creating a new cultural balance. The positions of different requirements intersect once more on the site. The association of significances has ingrained itself in the phenomenology of the place.

The first phase was characterized by opposing positions and a lack of goals in the search for the place's future purpose. After eight and a half months increasingly clear structures crystallized. The empiricism has produced a statistical majority picture and transformed it into a city-planning seeding-tray. The present consensus illustrates the three positions of new beginning, reconstruction and remembrance. By combining the outcome of the ImagineNY workshop with the NYNV principles, the averaged need for built and open spaces and the envisioned mixture of multi-functional uses, the blueprint for the Masterplan of a new World Trade Center lies just there (**fig. 13-16**, p. 50-53).

In the mutual struggle for this consensus is expressed the pristine form of democracy. The dominant principle of power and powerlessness was disabled for a brief time. During this phase the phenomenon of self-determination and determination of purpose led to a renewal of a communitarian ideal.

Even though Ground Zero/New York seems like desert wasteland or one of the many Ground Zeros in the deserts of Nevada, the naivety of this idea of the innocent soil has been lost. A new beginning is impossible. The hole is never empty and can never be filled. This change in mentality over time would have required a stronger assimilation process in order to confront the *newness* of this situation, namely the historical demands of the place, and to test strategies appropriate for this day and age. If there is something to criticize, it has to be the speed with which New York returns to everyday business dealings and fortunes. It remains to be investigated whether the first phase of this historical process has left traces in the structures of social logic.

postscript

In July 2002 the first *professional* designs by a New York-based architectural office were presented at a public conference organized by the LMDC and the Civic Alliance. More than 5,000 people from New York participated, debated in randomly constituted groups, and discredited the plans at hand as inadequate and banal.

In August 2002 the LMDC and NYNV (a member of the Public Process) proclaimed an international competition for ideas. Seven offices were invited to submit entries to a subsequent competition for the design of a master-plan. Amongst these offices were those of Norman Foster, Daniel Libeskind, Peter Eisenman, Richard Meier, SOM and THINK Team with Shigeru Ban, Rafael Viñoly and Fred Schwartz (a member NYNV).

Over the course of the competition SOM withdrew its entry. Larry Silverstein, who had already commissioned SOM as a planner, complained to LMDC and demanded that the planning for the reconstruction be his responsibility since it was after all his money, the money the insurance companies would be making available to him for the reinstatement process.

Unfazed by Silverstein's initiative, LMDC chose two finalists: THINK Team and Studio Daniel Libeskind. At the end of February the members of LMDC chose THINK Team's design as presented by Rafael Viñoly. However, Governor Pataki, who had personally empowered the LMDC, intervened and overruled this decision by choosing the design of Studio Daniel Libeskind as the sole winner. At this moment all the pessimistic and critical voices which suspected that the much-heralded fair, public and transparent process was nothing but a cover for the machinations of two men, Governor George E. Pataki and Larry Silverstein, were confirmed.

However, if we take a close look at the plans, the sketch previously developed by the public process emerges from it: various uses, the old grid pattern, the ratio between built-up space and open space, footprints as a memorial, revitalization through work, dwellings, traffic, museums, theatres, exhibition spaces, a documentation centre and not least an Islamic center.

Today the site of the World Trade Center comes across as a patchwork of different demands and influences. In the design of the buildings an attempt has been made to use a spectrum of big names to achieve the most far-reaching possible symbolic intensity, by involving Daniel Libeskind, Norman Foster, Frank Gehry and Santiago Calatrava for example. Thus the observer of current developments is under a double deception: firstly, the buildings being created now with their seemingly symbolic character are covering up the process underlying them; and secondly, this covering up helps critics to feel justified in their claim that the public was not going to have any say in the new plans right from the start. Unfortunately the surface does not accord the implicit phenomena the corresponding reference and only those who take a close look will be able to read in the texts of the built architecture.

img. 1: Fence at Ground Zero // **img. 2–7:** Temporary Memorials

img. 8: Ground Zero, Sep. 23 2001 // **img. 9–14:** Meetings at NYNV, R.Dot, CB#1, Civic Alliance

GS   Governmental Sector
PP   Public Process
LS   Larry Silverstein
PA   Port Authority
GP   Governor Pataki
VF   Victims' Families
MB   Mayor Bloomberg
CA   Civic Alliance
        LMDC

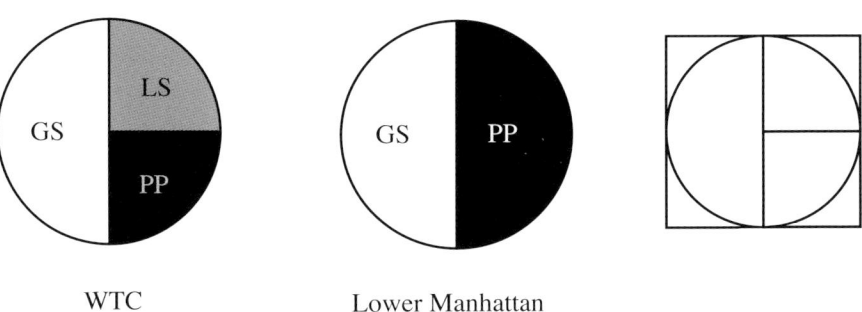

WTC   Lower Manhattan

fig. 5: Parties involved in the rebuilding process

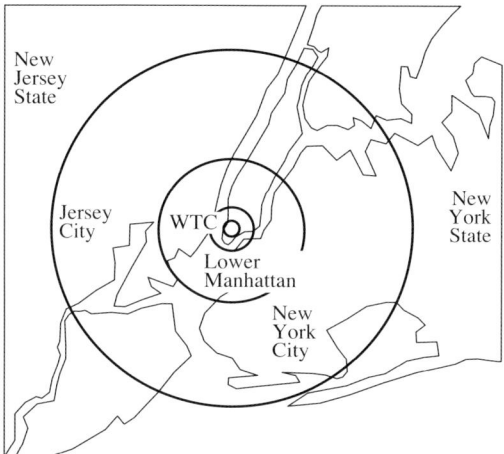

fig. 4: Epicenter WTC

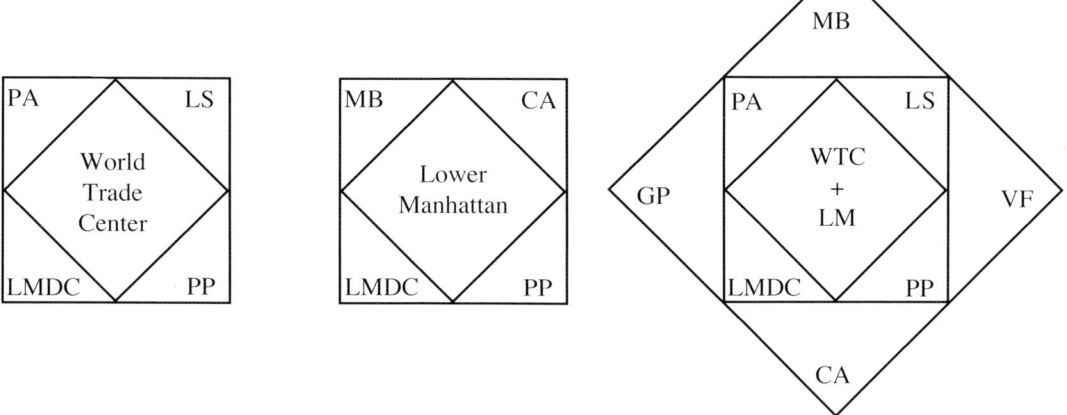

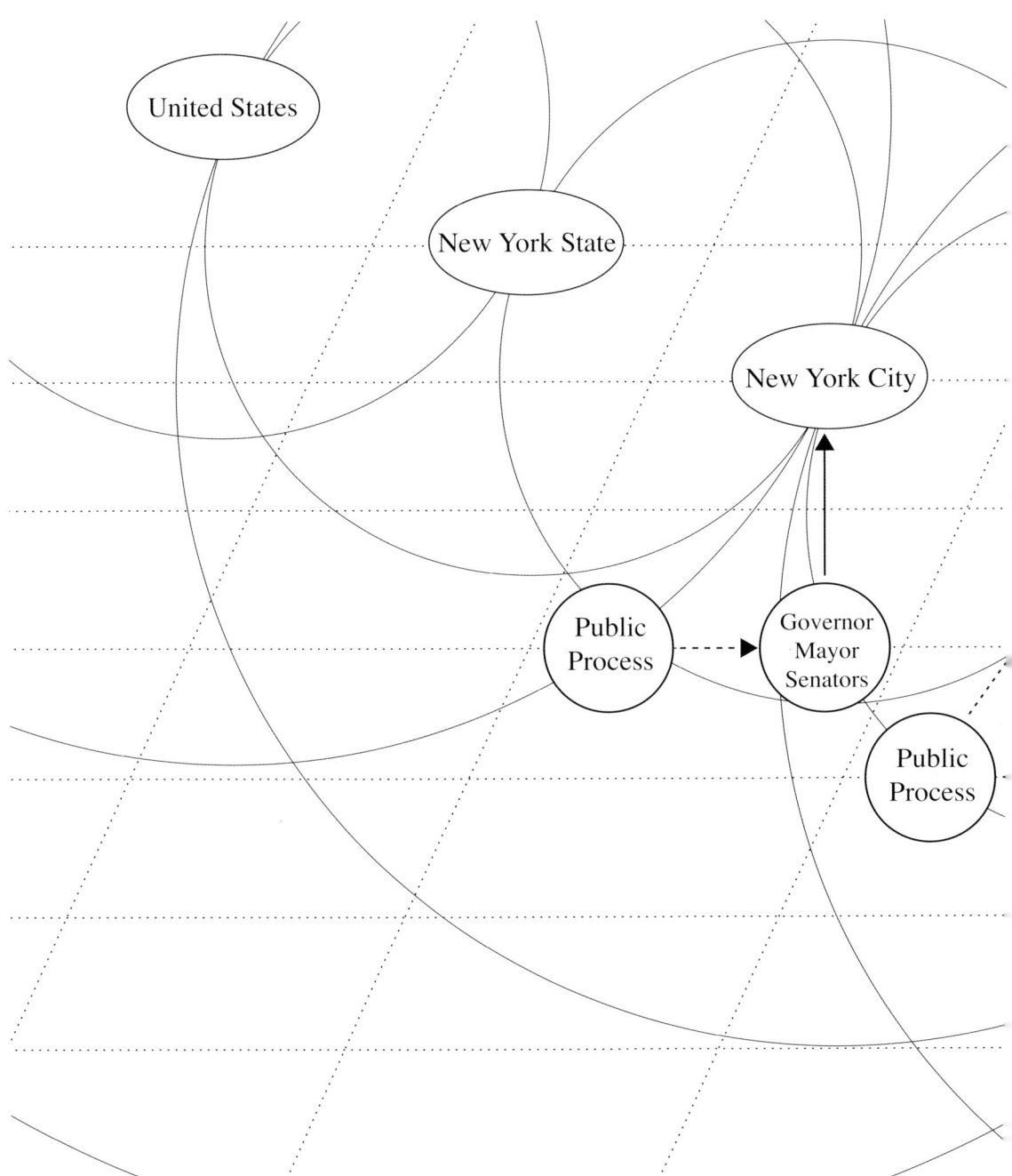

fig. 6: Public Process and its influence on the rebuilding process with regard to scale and scope

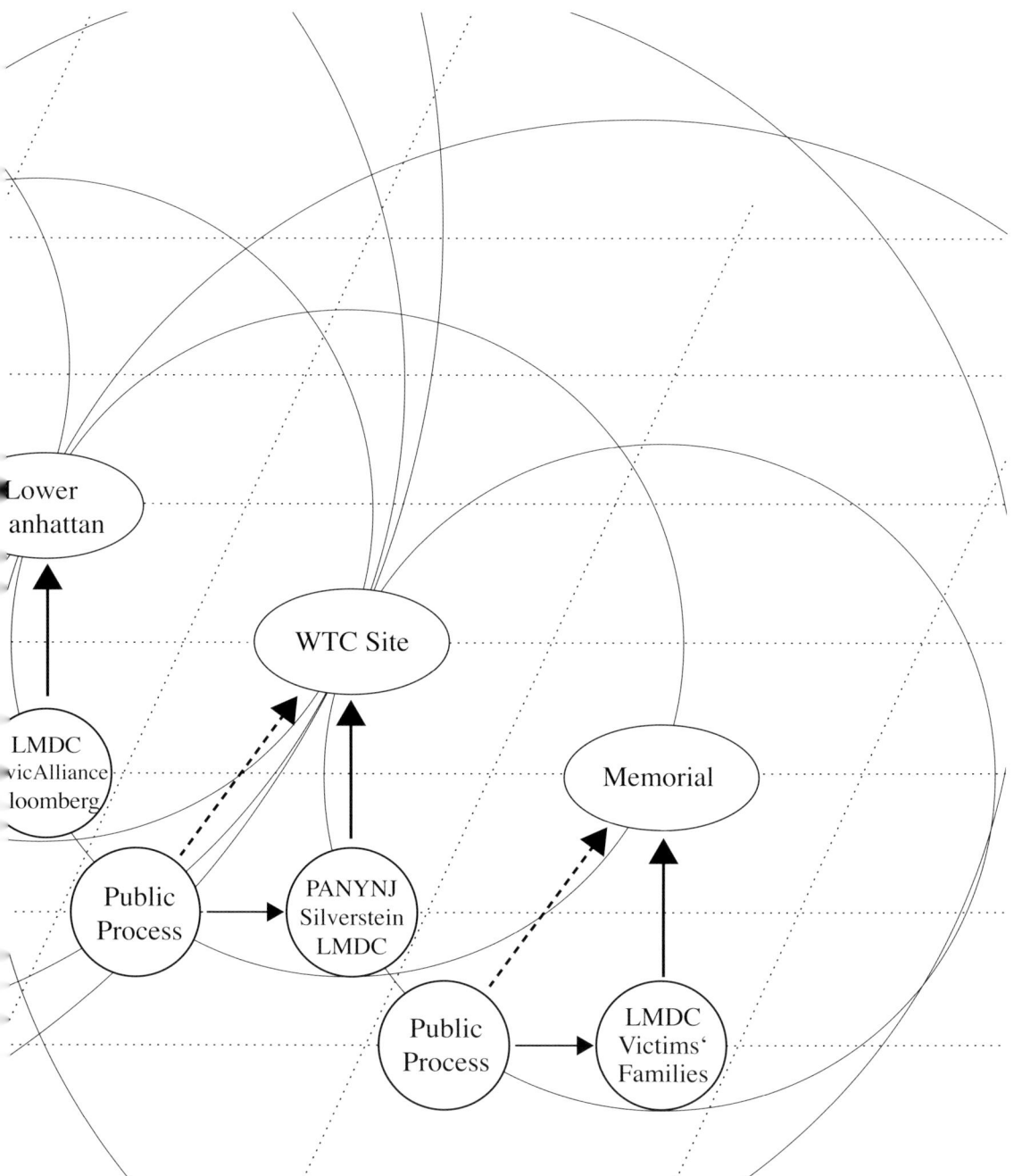

Lower
anhattan

WTC Site

Memorial

LMDC
vicAlliance
loomberg

Public
Process

PANYNJ
Silverstein
LMDC

Public
Process

LMDC
Victims'
Families

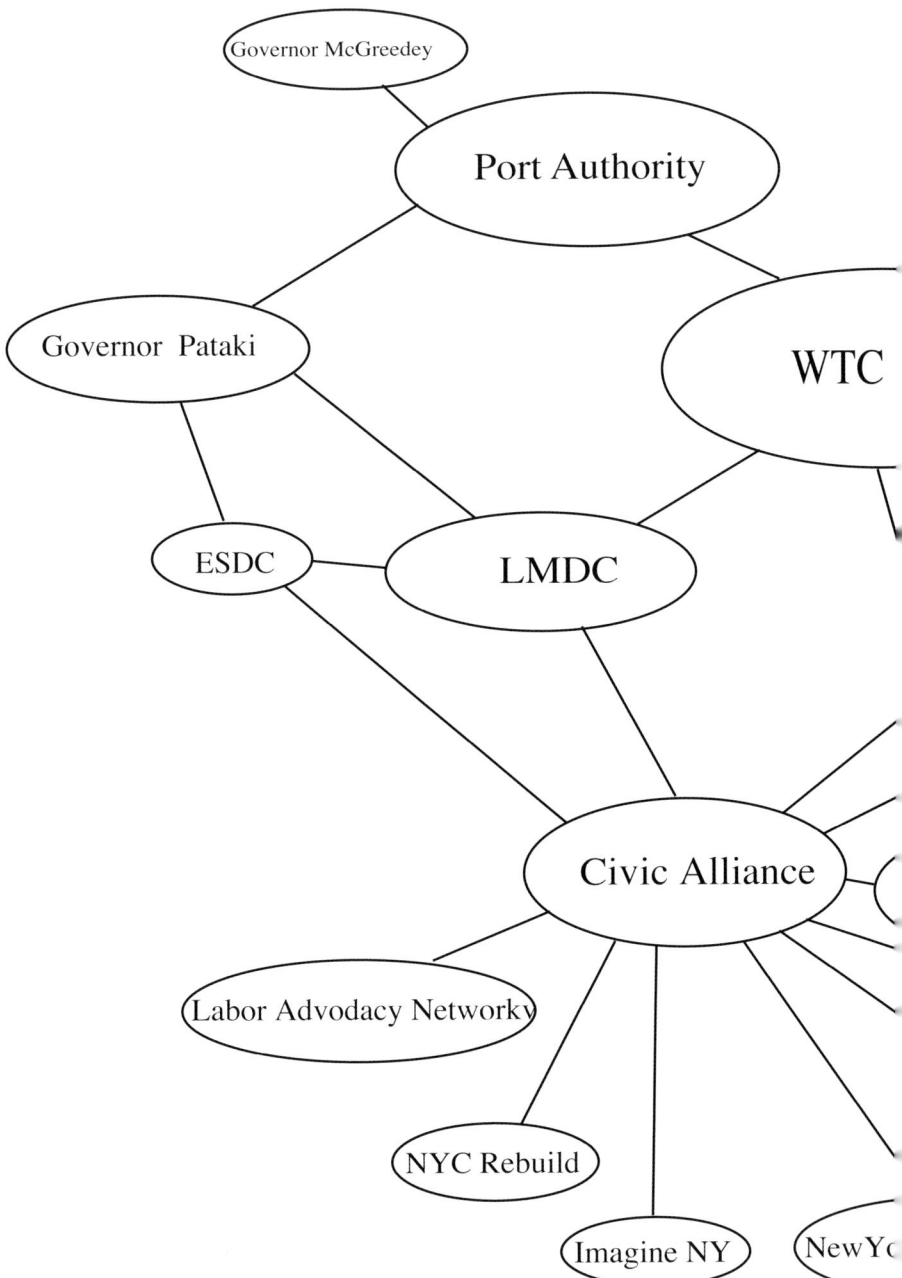

fig. 7: Entanglement of groups, parties, institutions and individuals involved in the process

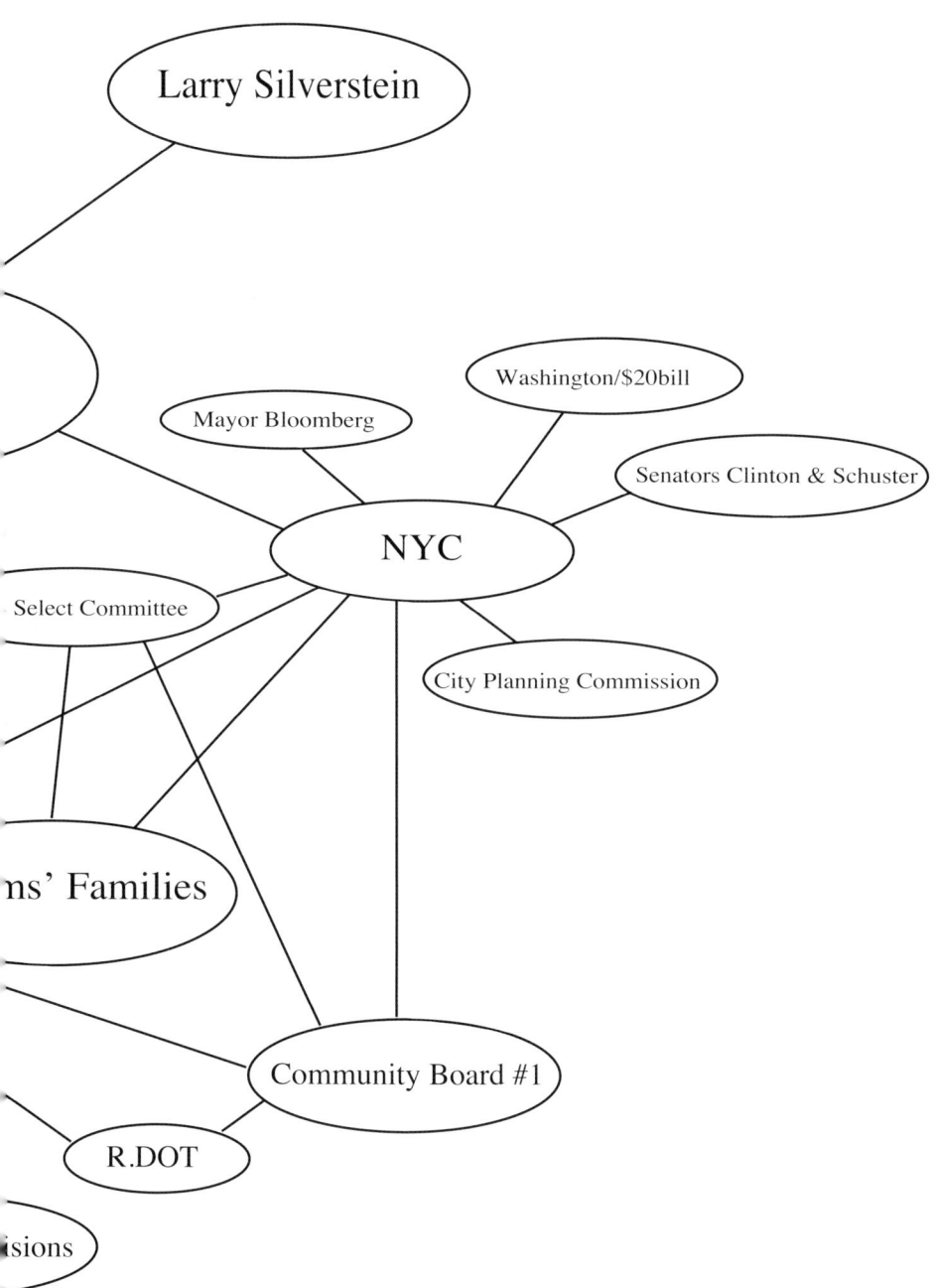

Larry Silverstein

Washington/$20bill

Mayor Bloomberg

Senators Clinton & Schuster

NYC

Select Committee

City Planning Commission

ns' Families

Community Board #1

R.DOT

isions

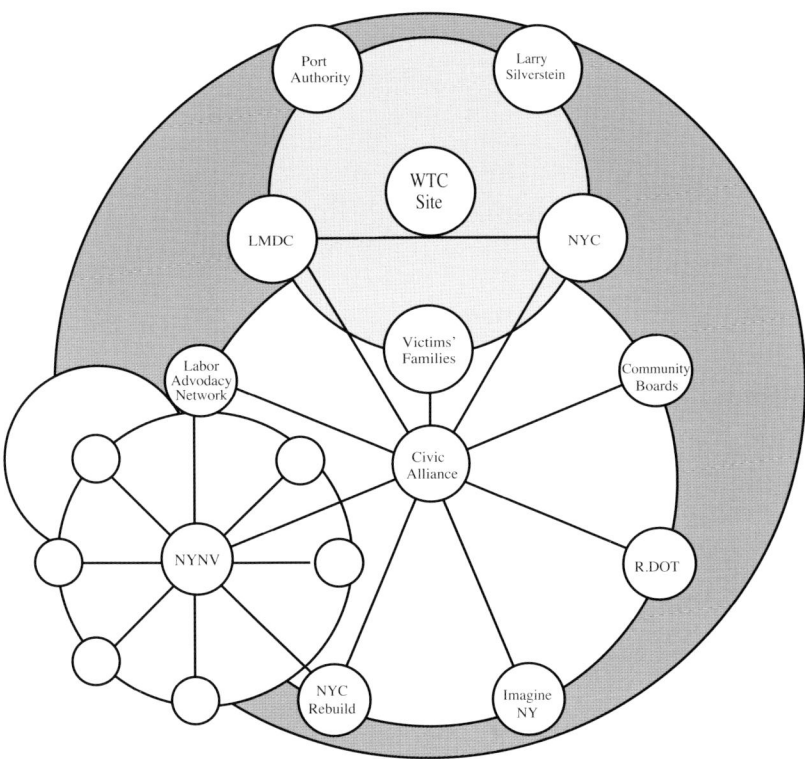

fig. 8: Every participating group is composed of various other participants

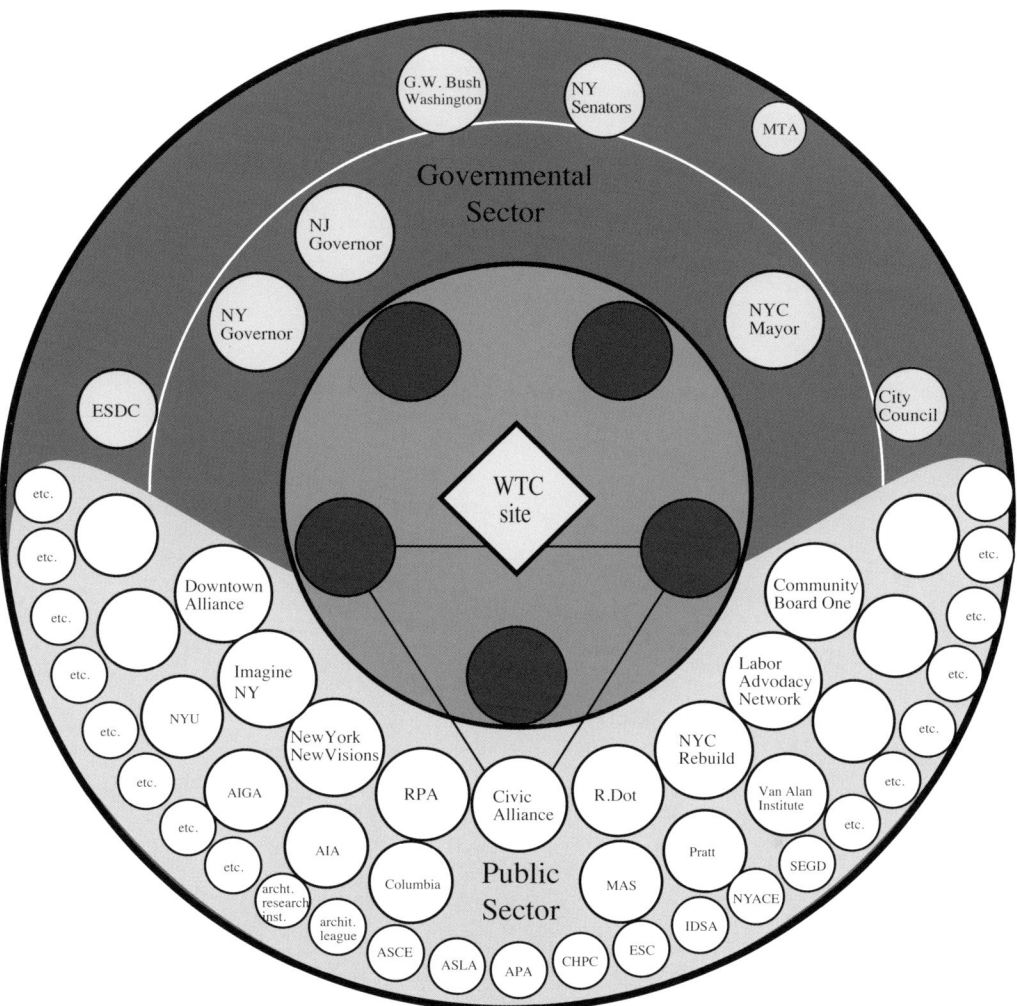

fig. 9: Classifying and assorting to either the public or the governmental sector

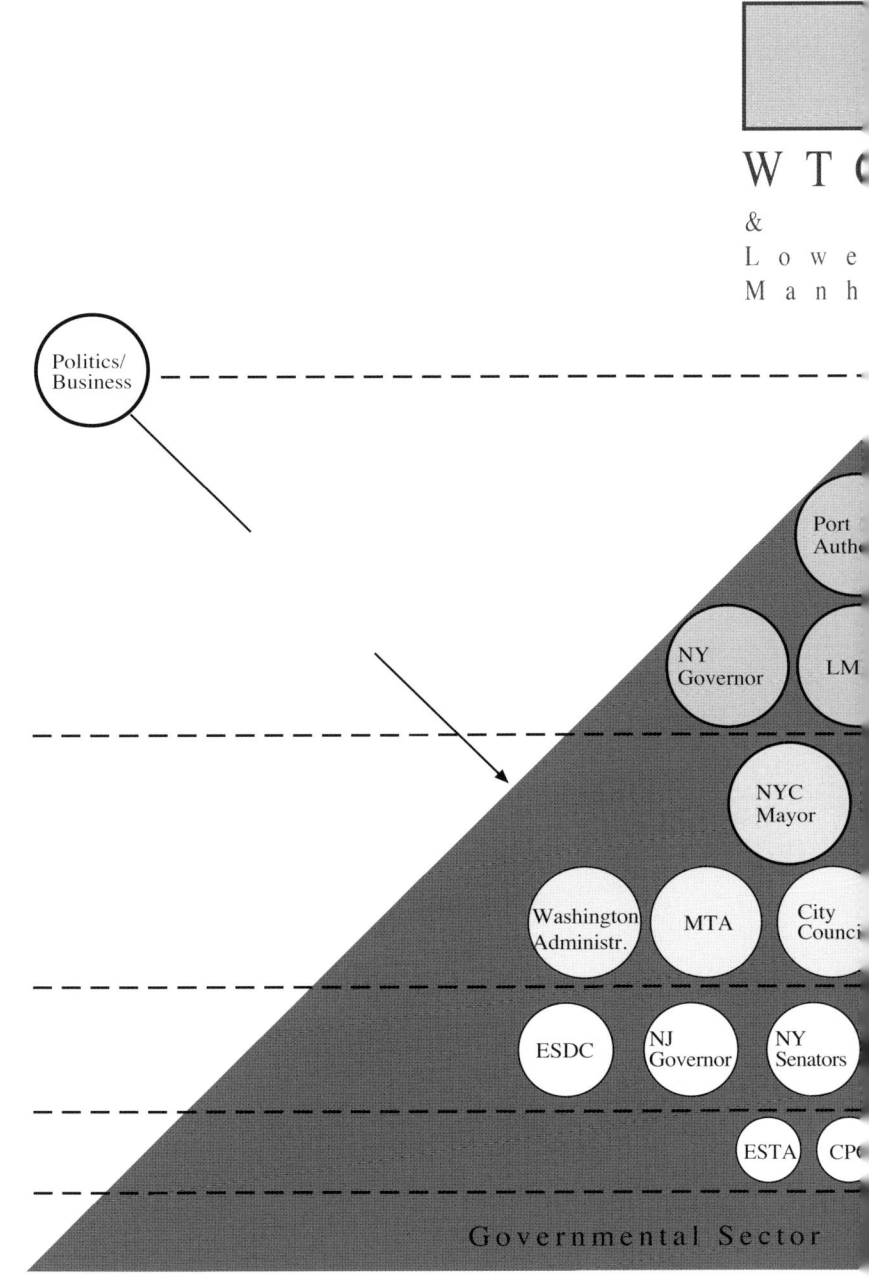

fig. 10: Input and importance to the rebuilding process // Sep. 2001 – May 2002

ite

n

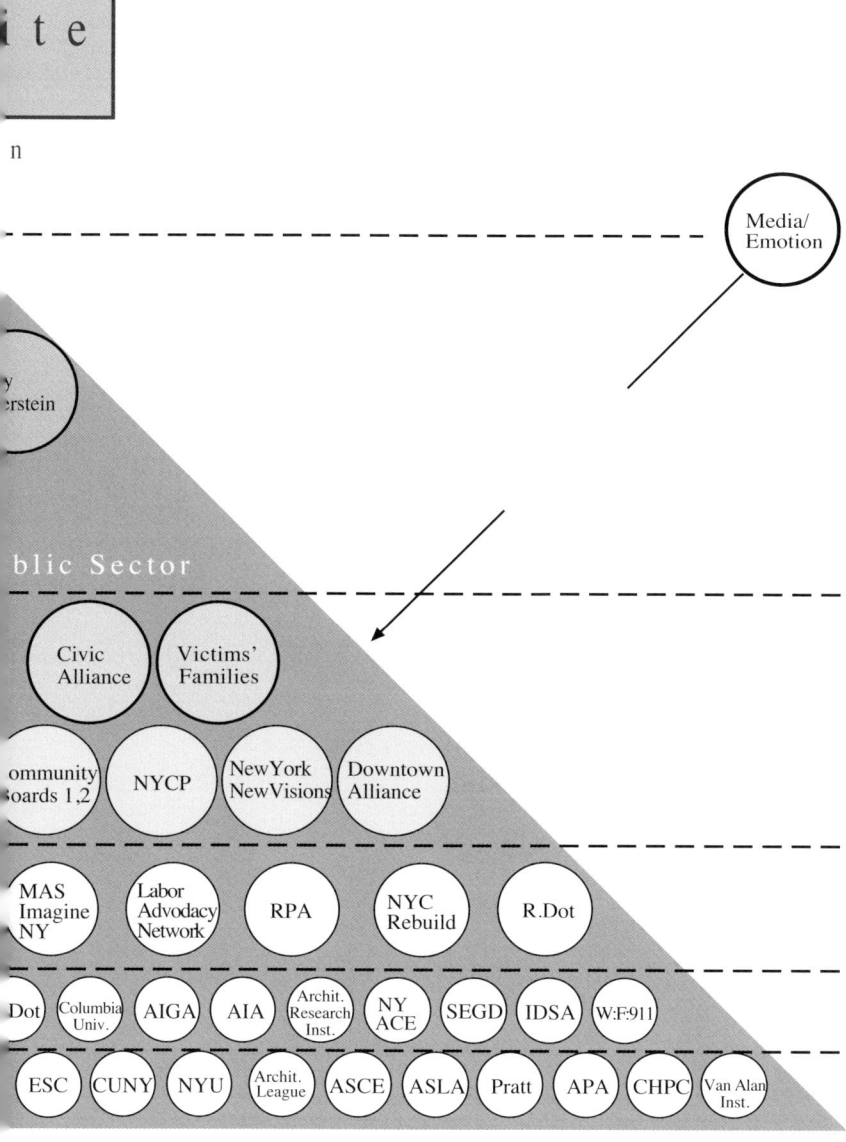

Media/
Emotion

y
erstein

blic Sector

Civic
Alliance

Victims'
Families

ommunity
oards 1,2

NYCP

New York
New Visions

Downtown
Alliance

MAS
Imagine
NY

Labor
Advodacy
Network

RPA

NYC
Rebuild

R.Dot

Dot

Columbia
Univ.

AIGA

AIA

Archit.
Research
Inst.

NY
ACE

SEGD

IDSA

W:F:911

ESC

CUNY

NYU

Archit.
League

ASCE

ASLA

Pratt

APA

CHPC

Van Alan
Inst.

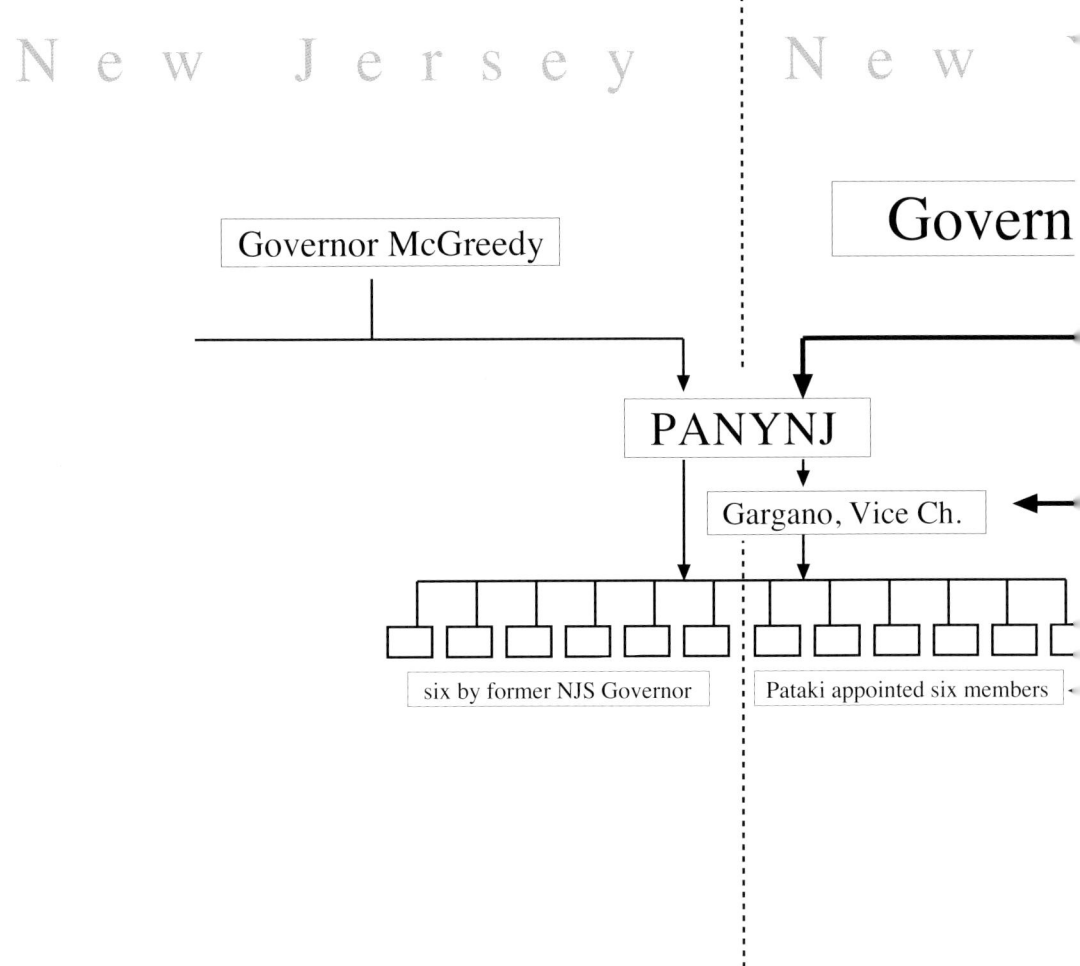

Governor McGreedy

Govern

PANYNJ

Gargano, Vice Ch.

six by former NJS Governor

Pataki appointed six members

fig. 11: Involvements of New York State Governor George E. Pataki

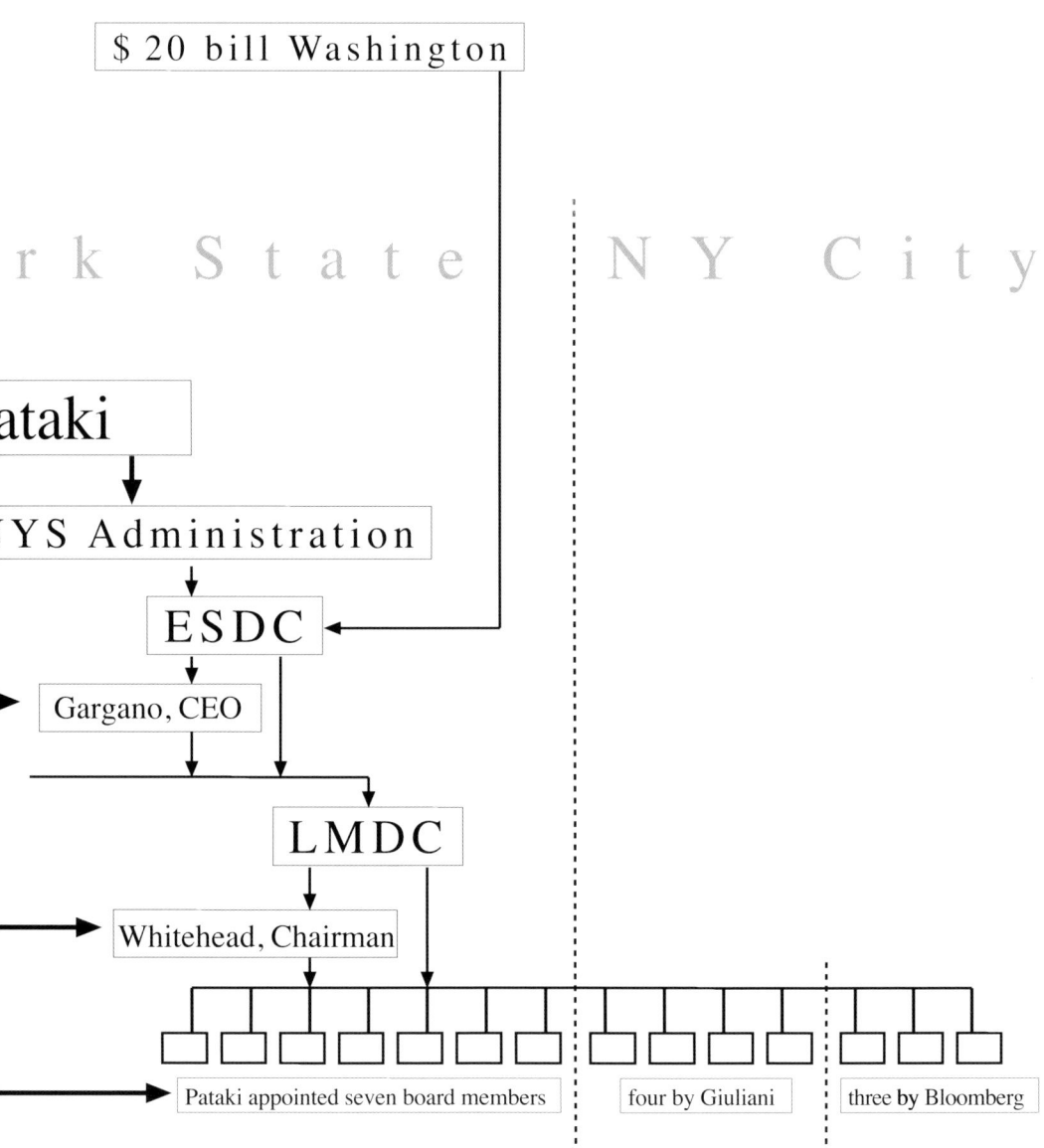

$ 20 bill Washington

r k S t a t e | N Y C i t y

ataki

NYS Administration

ESDC

Gargano, CEO

LMDC

Whitehead, Chairman

Pataki appointed seven board members

four by Giuliani

three by Bloomberg

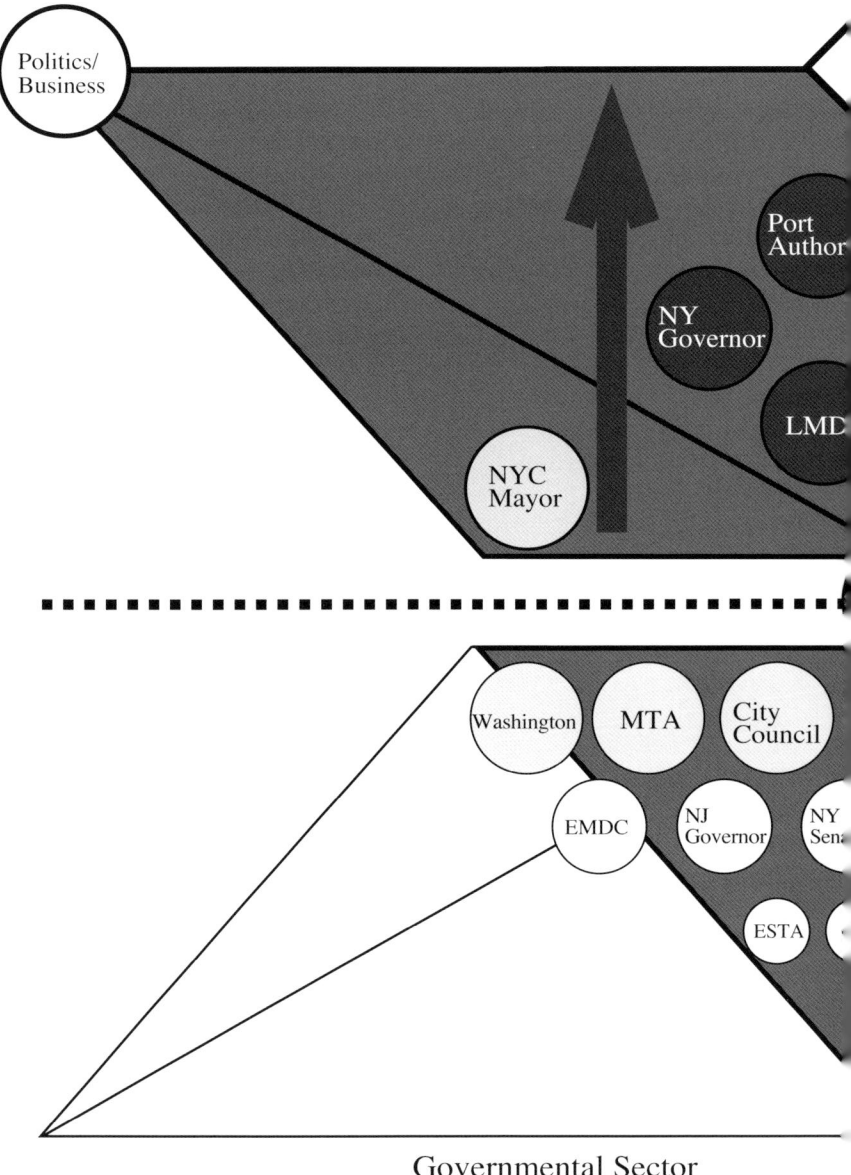

Governmental Sector

fig. 12: Future prospects of the public sector participating in the process // Jul. 2002 – 2011

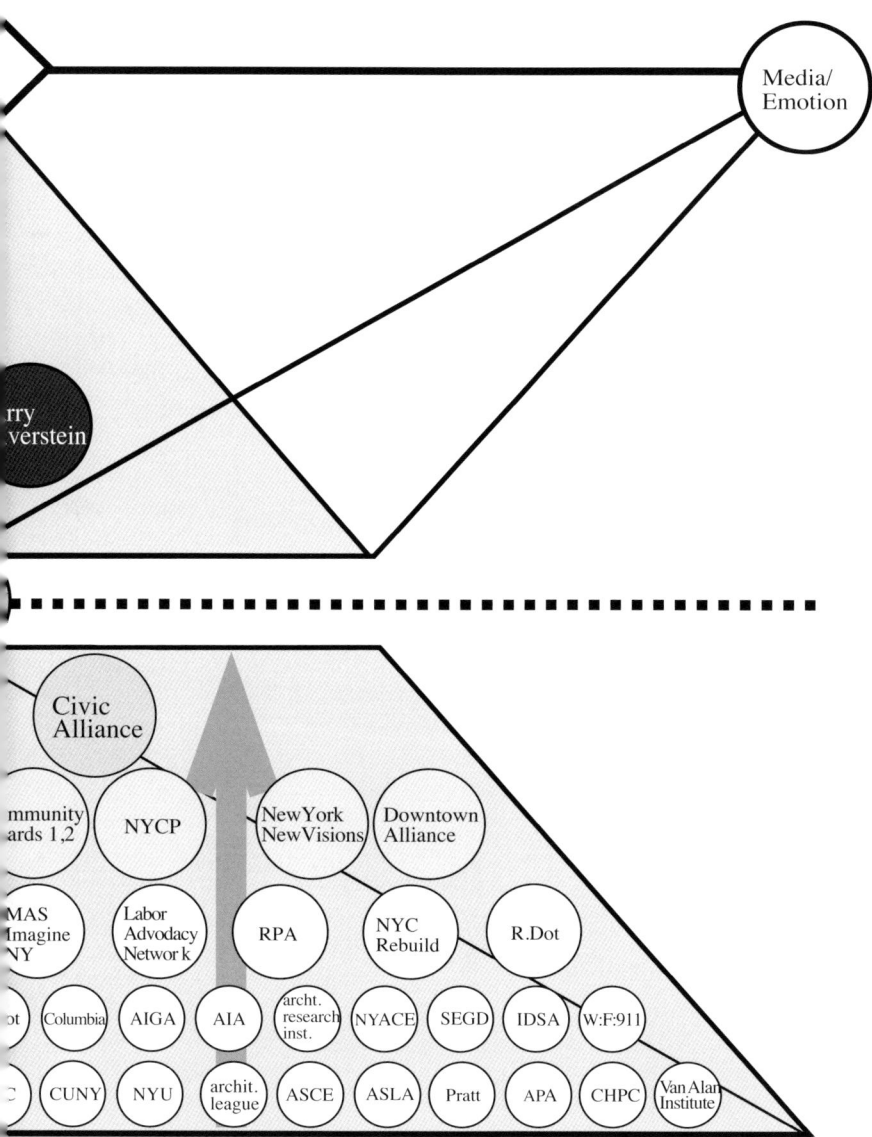

Media/
Emotion

rry
verstein

Civic
Alliance

mmunity
ards 1,2

NYCP

New York
New Visions

Downtown
Alliance

MAS
magine
NY

Labor
Advocacy
Network

RPA

NYC
Rebuild

R.Dot

ot

Columbia

AIGA

AIA

archt.
research
inst.

NYACE

SEGD

IDSA

W:F:911

C

CUNY

NYU

archit.
league

ASCE

ASLA

Pratt

APA

CHPC

Van Alan
Institute

Public Sector

```
Imagine New York
Workshop Municipal Art Society
Snug Harbour - Staten Island

two women facilitating the workshop
and ten participants,
eight women and two men (including me)_ age between
35 and 55 years_ all white_ middle class_

what have we lost?
3000 people; security; loved ones; focus on previous
agendas; parents of thousands of children; friends
and neighbours; chunk of the skyline; freedom; sense
of isolation and aloofness; comfort level; sense that
we are admired throughout the world; holidays that
will never be the same because of family members we
lost; certainty that we or our people will come home
at night; a sense of permanence; we may not have
liked the towers, but didn't want them to disappear;
skills, experience; trust in others

how have we changed?
economy has suffered, particularly the culturals;
back to same routine; more sceptical, fragile, vul-
nerable; vocabulary is different; increase in a sense
of community; more focus on living and loving in the
moment; more cautious and more courageous; knowing
it can happen here and not just to the other guy;
an awakening recognition of our place in the world;
tolerance for denial of civilrights and ignoring of
policies that might otherwise be more scrutinized
under the guise of nationalism; more angry and more
grateful; a motivation to make each day count; in-
teraction among unfamiliar communities; became more
aware of tragedies somewhere alse in the world; we're
```

fig. 13: Municipal Art Society: Imagine NY, Workshop Series Mar. – May 2002 (Transcript) sadder, more alert to beauty; a lot of people have demonstrated a sense of patriotism, a lot of people with post-traumatic stress and the willingness to seek mental help; a lot of people more cynical; more respect for civil servants

what should be done?
the most effective change will arise from the grassroots, from the ground up rather than top down; find a way to get muslims, jews, christians, agnostics, atheists together; make it a memorial day of commemoration; build an extremly spacious garden, with benches and many paths; built buildings above ground, with labyrinth, mosaics; that the tragedy never be trivialized; and the lives that were taken never be lost from our consciousness; increase transportation; have a monument to honour, remember and respect the people who were lost; the federal government should take over a good portion of the site, the footprints, to create a cemetary; I envision a circle as a symbol of connectedness; a huge prayer room; a book with life stories of each person; in addition to the site there should be a memorial at fresh kills; the remains should be returned to the wtc site; new buildings should consider the safety of people; a concert, music; museum; a forest, a tree for each person at fresh kills; something of the height at the site; a museum of war and peace; to give our children hope for the future themes _spectacular memorial at the WTC site/_sacred ground/_cover large area/_fresh kills/_remembrance, meditations, sharing knowledge/_ adequately remembering the men and women/_hope/_memorial should do something to teach

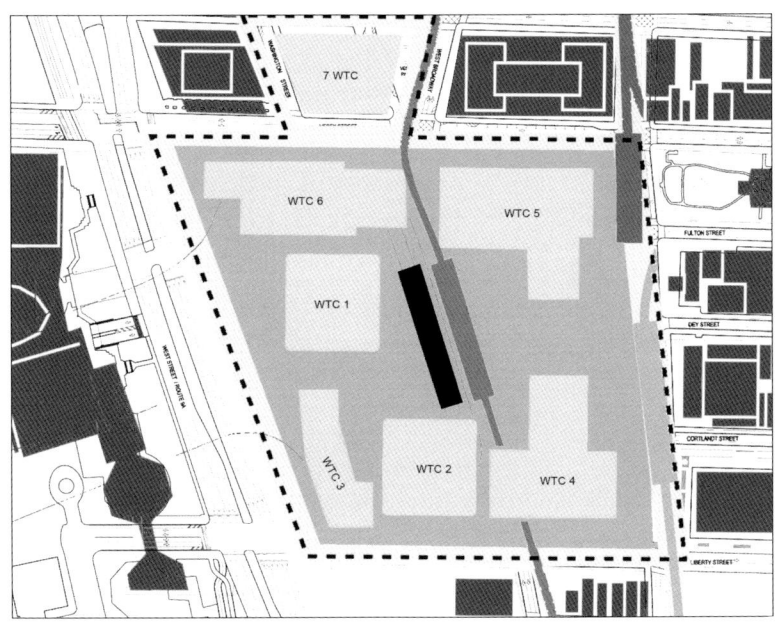

fig. 14: Site Plan, World Trade Center, Arch. Minoru Yamasaki, 1971 – 2001

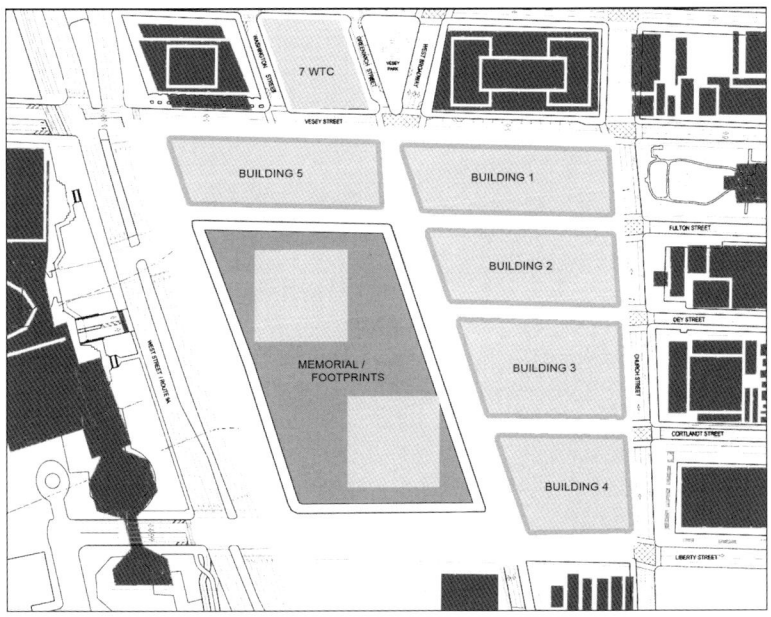

fig. 15: Site Plan, According to consensus reached through the Public Process, 2002

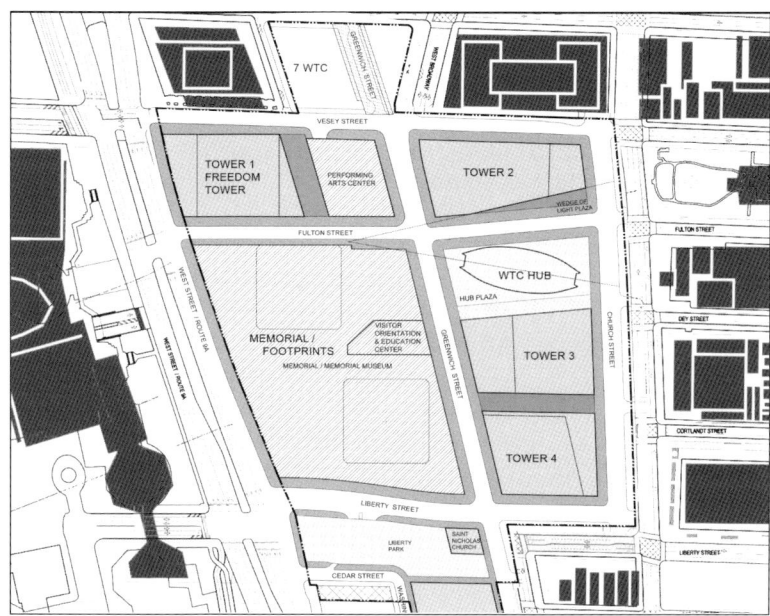

fig. 16: Site Plan, Masterplan, Designed by Studio Libeskind, 2003

nachtrag

Im Juli 2002 wurden auf einer von der LMDC und der Civic Alliance ausgerichteten öffentlichen Konferenz die ersten *professionellen* Entwürfe eines New Yorker Architekturbüros vorgestellt. Mehr als 5.000 New Yorker nahmen daran teil, diskutierten in zufällig gemischten Runden und diskreditierten die vorliegenden Pläne als unzureichend und banal.

Im August 2002 riefen LMDC und NYNV (eine öffentliche Initiative) einen internationalen Ideenwettbewerb aus. Sieben Büros wurden zu einem anschließenden Wettbewerb für den Entwurf des Masterplans eingeladen. Darunter waren Norman Foster, Daniel Libeskind, Peter Eisenman, Richard Meier, SOM, sowie THINK Team mit Shigeru Ban, Rafael Viñoly und Fred Schwartz (Mitglied von NYNV).

Im Verlauf des Wettbewerbs zogen SOM ihren Beitrag zurück. Larry Silverstein, der SOM bereits als Planer beauftragt hatte, beschwerte sich bei der LMDC und forderte, dass die Planung des Wiederaufbaus in seiner Verantwortung läge, da es ja schließlich um sein Geld ginge. Das Geld, das ihm die Versicherungen für den Wiederaufbau zur Verfügung stellen würden.

Unberührt von Silversteins Vorstoß wählte die LMDC zwei Finalisten aus: THINK Team und Studio Daniel Libeskind. Ende Februar entschieden sich die Mitglieder der LMDC für den von Rafael Viñoly präsentierten Entwurf des THINK Teams. Doch Gouverneur Pataki, der selber die LMDC einberufen hatte, intervenierte und überstimmte diese Entscheidung, indem er den Entwurf vom Studio Daniel Libeskind als alleinigen Sieger kürte. In diesem Moment fanden all die pessimistischen und kritischen Stimmen ihre Bestätigung, die den viel beschworenen fairen, öffentlichen und transparenten Prozess immer schon als Deckmantel für das Wirken von zwei Männern, Gouverneur George E. Pataki und Larry Silverstein, vermutet hatten.

Wenn man aber genau auf den Bebauungsplan schaut, dann scheint daraus die Skizze hervor, die zuvor durch den öffentlichen Prozess entwickelt wurde: Verschiedene Nutzungen, das alte Straßenraster, Verhältnis von Bebauung zu Freiflächen, Footprints als Mahnmal, Wiederbelebung durch Arbeiten, Wohnen, Verkehr, Museum, Theater, Ausstellungsflächen, ein Dokumentationszentrum, sowie die Einrichtung eines Islamic Centers.

Heute präsentiert sich das Gelände des World Trade Centers als Flickenteppich verschiedener Ansprüche und Einflüsse. Beim Design der Gebäude wurde versucht, durch ein Spektrum großer Namen eine möglichst weitreichende symbolische Strahlkraft zu erzielen, beispielsweise durch Daniel Libeskind, Norman Foster, Frank Gehry oder Santiago Calatrava. Somit unterliegt der Betrachter der gegenwärtigen Entwicklungen einer doppelten Täuschung: Erstens verdeckt die jetzt entstehende symbolisch anmutende Bebauung die ihr zugrunde liegenden Prozesse. Und zweitens, durch das Verdecken verhilft man der Kritik zur Berechtigung, dass die Öffentlichkeit von Anfang an kein Mitspracherecht bei der Neuplanung haben sollte. Leider erweist die Oberfläche den impliziten Phänomenen keine entsprechende Referenz und nur wer genau hinschaut, kann diese in den Texten der gebauten Architektur nachlesen.

Es bleibt die Frage offen, ob die veränderte Rolle, die der Öffentlichkeit jetzt beigemessen wird, die Einschätzung ihrer bisherigen Bedeutung diskreditiert, und die Anwort der kulturellen Reaktion in dem historischen und symbolischen Zusammenhang anders ausfällt, als wir es gerne angenommen hätten.

In Anlehnung an Heideggers Phänomenologie ließe sich eine ästhetische Konzeptualisierung des Prozesses und der Rolle der Öffentlichkeit entwickeln: Das Kunstwerk als Konkretion von Sinn verdichtet die Lebenszusammenhänge des Daseins. Wenn ein Ort mit solcher Gewalt aus der Vorstellung seiner konventionalisierten Erscheinung herausgerissen wird wie die Türme und das Areal des World Trade Centers, dann bedarf es einer kulturellen Anstrengung, ihn wieder in der Gesellschaft zu verankern und die Leere zu überwinden.

Der Architekt Rem Koolhaas hatte im Oktober 2001 davon gesprochen, dass es zu früh sei für Architekten, ihre Entwürfe zu präsentieren, man müsste „abwarten, bis sich eine neue kulturelle Balance entwickelt hätte." Diese Bedingung ist nun erfüllt. Der intensive öffentliche Prozess hat dazu beigetragen, eine neue kulturelle Balance herzustellen. Auf dem Grundstück kreuzen sich wieder die Positionen unterschiedlicher Bedürfnisse. Der Sinnzusammenhang hat sich in die Phänomenologie des Ortes eingeschrieben.

Die erste Phase war durch konträre Positionen und Ziellosigkeit auf der Suche nach der zukünftigen Bestimmung des Ortes geprägt. Nach achteinhalb Monaten haben sich immer klarere Strukturen herausgebildet. Die Empirie hat ein statistisches Mehrheitsbild erzeugt und in einen stadtplanerischen Setzkasten umgewandelt. Der vorliegende Konsens illustriert die drei Positionen von Neuanfang, Wiederaufbau und

Erinnerung. Bei der Überlagerung des Imagine NY-Protokolls, den Prinzipien von NYNV und dem gemittelten Plan für die Flächenverteilung und Bebauung des WTC Geländes (**fig. 13-16**, S. 50-53) ergibt sich eine hinreichend genaue Blaupause für den Entwurf eines neuen World Trade Centers.

In dem gleichberechtigten Ringen um diesen Konsens zeigt sich die genuine Form von Demokratie. Das herrschende Prinzip von Macht und Ohnmacht war für kurze Zeit außer Kraft gesetzt. In dieser Phase hat das Phänomen der Selbst- und Sinnbestimmung zu einer Erneuerung eines gemeinschaftlichen Ideals geführt.

Obwohl Ground Zero/New York anmutet wie wüstes Brachland oder eins der vielen Ground Zeros in den Wüsten Nevadas ist die Naivität dieser Vorstellung vom unschuldigen Boden verloren. Es lässt sich nicht neu anfangen. Das Loch wird niemals leer und niemals zu füllen sein. Diese mentalitätsgeschichtliche Wende hätte eines stärkeren Assimilierungsprozesses bedurft, um sich mit dem „Neuen" dieser Situation, nämlich der historischen Vorgabe des Ortes, auseinanderzusetzen und zeitgemäße Strategien zu erproben. Wenn es einen Kritikpunkt gibt, so ist es die Geschwindigkeit, mit der New York zu alltäglichen Geschäften und Geschicken zurückkehrt. Es bleibt zu untersuchen, ob die erste Phase dieses historischen Prozesses Spuren in den Strukturen gesellschaftlicher Logik hinterlassen hat.

Die Port Authority sieht sich als verantwortlich für die Entscheidung eines Masterplanes für das Gelände des World Trade Centers und hat keine Jury und keinen internationalen Wettbewerb einberufen. Dieses Vorgehen hat erstaunlich wenig öffentliche Kritik hervorgebracht.

die wüste

Es ist an dieser Stelle angebracht auf den experimentellen Charakter der amerikanischen Vergangenheit und ihrer kulturellen und gesellschaftlichen Entwicklung hinzuweisen. Der Wüste als ästhetischer Kategorie entspricht die Vorstellung der Freiheit, sich in der Gesetzlosigkeit einer Gegenwart zu beweisen und auf vermeintlich neutralem Boden Grenzen zu überschreiten. Die Wüste war seit jeher der Ort der Versuchung und Suche nach sich selbst. Das Western-Genre, die Zündung nuklearer Sprengsätze in Nevada oder die Erfindung des Road Movies, seit den biblischen Erzählungen finden Genesis und Katharsis in der Abwesenheit und Abgeschiedenheit der Wüsten statt.

Als ich nach New York kam, war ich auf der Suche nach einer eigenen, gestalterischen Konzeption. Die Anwesenheit und die Recherche vor Ort zeigten mir, dass diese Art der subjektiven Stellungnahme zu diesem Zeitpunkt noch unangebracht war. In New York hatte sich eine Form des gemeinschaftlichen Entwerfens dieser Aufgabe angenommen. Die demokratische Konsequenz auf die Ereignisse des 11. Septembers hatte den Anschein, dem Wesen der Architektur als gesellschaftlichem Medium zu entsprechen. Diese Arbeit habe ich mit meiner Mitarbeit in den Arbeitsgruppen zu unterstützen gesucht.

Es wäre eine wertvolle Aufgabe mit experimentellem Charakter gewesen, den öffentlichen Entwurfsprozess in dieser Intensität und Dimension fortzuführen. Es wäre die einzigartige Antwort auf das *unprecedented event* gewesen. Der Übergang von der ersten zur zweiten Phase zeigt, dass die Qualität des öffentlichen Prozesses gleichzeitig zu seinem Nachteil gereicht, weil die Offenheit und umfassende Anteilnahme in den Konflikt der Richtungslosigkeit mündet. In diesem Stadium wurde die begonnene Arbeit unterbrochen und in herkömmlicher Weise verfahren, d. h., dass Autoritäten ihre Kompetenzen delegieren. Hätte das Funktionsschema des öffentlichen Konsens nicht als Entwurfsvorlage dienen können, auf der sich der öffentliche Prozess weiter als Planer betätigt, um damit auf der Suche nach dem *Wesen der Aufgabe* zu bleiben?

Aus den bisherigen Grafiken lässt sich eine Situation entwerfen, in der sich die Entscheidungen für die Zukunft des WTC-Geländes auf höherer Ebene abspielen werden, unter Ausschluss der Öffentlichkeit (**fig. 12**, S. 48/49). Von Anfang an war die Frage der Macht ein zentrales Thema jeder Diskussion und es bestand die Hoffnung, dass es diese Ausscheidung nicht geben würde, mit anderen Worten, dass New York nicht zum „business as usual" zurückkehren würde. Eine Mauer trennt die Öffentlichkeit von dem Prozedere und ersetzt ihre Aktion durch ihre Reaktion.

Nach der Darstellung dieser kritischen Faktoren schwindet der Eindruck der Bedeutsamkeit des Public Process. Es ist jedoch nicht die reale Kräfteverteilung, sondern die inhaltliche Substanz, die qualitative Einflussnahme, die ausschlaggebend für die Beurteilung sein sollte: Die Arbeit an einem kollektiven Gedächtnis des 11. Septembers, die Gemeinschaft freiwilliger Tätigkeit und die Formulierung eines gesellschaftlichen Konsens bilden die Voraussetzung für weitere Prozesse um die Zukunft von Ground Zero.

damit die Diskussionen konkreter Fragen der Gestaltung bezüglich des Geländes und der Neubebauung abgelöst.

Den Vorwurf der Therapie beurteile ich im Angesicht der produktiven Arbeit, der Intelligenz der Initiativen und meiner Erfahrung 2002 vor Ort als unzutreffend. Sicherlich geht es auch um die Bewältigung im Sinne psychischer Prozesse: Schmerz, Trauer, Ohnmacht, Trauma, Verlust, existenzielle Bedrohung und veränderte Wahrnehmung. Aber die konstruktive Natur des Prozesses konstituiert sich durch die Notwendigkeit, Rezession und Arbeitslosigkeit zu beseitigen. Von der These der Therapie ließe sich in Bezugnahme auf den Zeitgeist von einer gemeinsamen Marketingstrategie von Politik und Wirtschaft (*Public Private Partnership*) sprechen, und damit zu der These des politischen Theaters und der Marginalität der öffentlichen Einflussnahme überleiten.

Das übermäßige Verhältnis wirtschaftlicher Interessen zeigt sich wie folgt:
– Die Kommission der Lower Manhattan Development Corporation ist mit Personen besetzt, die aus den Chefetagen großer Wirtschaftsunternehmen kommen und enge Kontakte zur Politik pflegen. Nur ein Mitglied arbeitet in kommunalpolitischen Zusammenhängen.
– Die Port Authority ist zwar eine staatliche Gesellschaft, aber wirtschaftlich vollkommen unabhängig vom Staat, und regiert deswegen ebenfalls nach marktwirtschaftlichen Prinzipien.
– Für Larry Silverstein geht es definitiv um sehr viel Geld.

Im November 2002 finden die Wahlen für das Amt des Gouverneures des Staates New York statt. Die Wiederwahl des Republikaners Pataki hängt in bedeutendem Maße davon ab, wie die Wähler den Erfolg seiner Arbeit beim Wie-

deraufbau einschätzen. Sein möglicher Demokratischer Gegenkandidat, Andrew M. Cuomo, versucht in seiner Wahlkampfstrategie genau in dieser Hinsicht die Rolle Patakis zu diskreditieren: Er wirft Pataki Führungslosigkeit in diesem Prozess vor und beanstandet, dass alles zu langsam vorangehe.

Die Langsamkeit resultiert aus den komplizierten Strukturen des Prozesses und ist Ergebnis der Beteiligung der vielen verschiedenen Gruppen. Dadurch, dass Cuomo hier Kritik schlägt, verkürzt er die Chancen auf einen umfassenden öffentlichen Prozess, was seiner Herkunft als Demokrat zu widersprechen scheint, und als reines Wahlkampfmanöver die geleistete Arbeit desavouiert. Obwohl der Vorwurf zweischneidig ist, reagiert Pataki mit seinen zwei führenden Institutionen und verschärft das Tempo. Es bleibt abzuwarten, ob es sich hierbei auch nur um ein politisches Manöver handelt, um dem politischen Gegner Wind aus den Segeln zu nehmen.

LMDC und Port Authority haben im April einen Zeitplan für die Entwicklung des WTC-Geländes vorgelegt, der in seiner unerwarteten Dichte erstaunt:
– Im Mai wurde in einem kurzfristig angekündigten Wettbewerb aus einem Feld von fünfzehn vorzüglich New Yorker Architekturbüros das Büro Beyer, Blinder und Belle ausgewählt.
– Bis 1. Juli sollen sie die ersten Entwürfe für einen Masterplan vorliegen, auch der Terminplan für die Durchführung eines Wettbewerbs für die Gedenkstätte soll bis dahin feststehen.
– Bis 1. September soll die Entscheidung für den endgültigen Entwurf getroffen sein.
– Im Dezember soll mit den Arbeiten begonnen werden.

Der erste Wettbewerb um die Zukunft von Ground Zero wurde unter der Hand durchgeführt.

Druck beschleunigte die öffentlichen Initiativen, auf der Suche nach zukunftsfähigen Lösungen schneller zu agieren als die institutionellen Seiten der Regierung und der Wirtschaft. Das unkontrollierte, spontane Engagement der Bürger hatte hier einen strukturellen Vorsprung, den es mit der Zeit allerdings wieder einbüßte.

Die Kritik des öffentlichen Prozesses ist durch die Diskussion auf unterschiedlichen Ebenen geprägt. Die *internationale* Kritik bemängelt vor allem das Fehlen einer Debatte, die sich mit den weltpolitischen Einordnungsversuchen und der selbstkritischen Ursachenforschung auseinandersetzt, wie z. B. der Auflösung des Paradoxon vom Wiederaufbau in Lower Manhattan und Afghanistan. Darüber hinaus geriert die unilaterale Abgegrenztheit und der Ausschluss internationaler Partizipation den Eindruck, dass sich Amerika im Anspruch der Internationalität selbst genüge.

Meine Beobachtungen und Erfahrungen zeigen, dass der Prozess niemanden ausschließt, dass aber kein Konzept existiert, nach dem die Integration der Weltöffentlichkeit organisiert werden könnte. Ich würde die internationale Perspektive bei der Diskussion ausklammern und für eine differenzierende Betrachtung einzelner Prozesse plädieren. So wie New York und Washington Zentren verschiedener Disposition darstellen, so handelt es sich auch um verschiedene Prozesse, die miteinander verknüpft sind. Dabei ergibt die Betrachtung elementarer Prozesse Einzelergebnisse, die sich unabhängig diskutieren lassen. Die Berechtigung der *regionalen* Perspektive liegt in der realen, materiellen Betroffenheit und der Vermeidung verfrühter Interpretationen in höchst kritischen politischen Zusammenhängen. Ich halte aus vorgenannten Gründen eine ausschließliche Diskussion über die Qualität des regionalen Prozesses für gerechtfertigt.

Die Kollaboration aller Beteiligten gilt als die Fortsetzung des „Geistes der Hilfsbereitschaft und der Gemeinschaft" in den Tagen nach dem 11. September. Das ist Konsens, das ist Politik und das ist sicherlich auch Pietät. Meinungsverschiedenheiten, schnöde Machtkämpfe oder politische Manöver sollen den Zusammenhalt und die Einigkeit nicht beeinträchtigen, die im Angesicht der Opfer, der Schrecken und der Folgen des Ereignisses angemessen erscheinen. Weil aber vieles so geblieben ist wie vorher, schwindet dieses Bekenntnis häufig zu einem dünnen Deckmantel, der nur noch vorgibt, diesen Anschein zu bewahren.

Nun gibt es mindestens zwei Lesarten, die sich Kritiker zueigen machen, um die Rolle der Öffentlichkeit in diesem Prozess zu hinterfragen: die eine vermutet eine Therapie, die andere eine Form des politischen Theaters. Ersteres meint, dass es sich bei der öffentlichen Teilnahme und Anteilnahme um eine Gesprächstherapie handelt, die einer ernsthaft zielgerichteten Absicht entbehrt und sich als der Versuch der Bewältigung des posttraumatischen Schreckens aufdecken lässt. Die andere sieht den Vorgang als Marionettentheater, in dem die Akteure der Freiwilligkeit von den Interessen der Mächtigen gesteuert werden, während der Anschein politischer und moralischer Akkuratesse im Sinne ihrer Instrumentalisierung aufrecht erhalten werden soll. Und letztendlich gibt es eine dritte, sozialphilosophische Diskussion, die den Zusammenhang zwischen *public process* und *common good*, also dem Einfluss und Anteil des öffentlichen Prozesses bei der Suche und der Bestimmung des Allgemeinwohls, historisch kritisch untersucht.

Die Existenz der Kritik begründet die Existenz des Objekts. Der Prozess, die Struktur inhaltlicher Suche, ist selbst zum Gegenstand inhaltlicher Auseinandersetzung geworden und hat abzuschätzen. Doch bis die letzte Entscheidung getroffen sein wird, wird noch genügend Zeit vergehen, um infrage zu stellen und neu zu überdenken. Der Erfolg des Public Process wird sich an dem Grad der Beteiligung in beiden Projekten, dem Gelände des WTC und den Planungen für Lower Manhattan, messen lassen müssen (**fig. 6**, S. 38/39).

Die nähere qualitative Untersuchung zeigt das kritische Verhältnis der Kräfteverteilung: Die Grafik (**fig. 10**, S. 44/45) ist unter Verwendung der Dreiecksform hierarchischer Strukturen weiterentwickelt. An der Spitze steht das WTC-Gelände mit der Frage nach der zukünftigen Nutzung. Der rechte Sektor zeigt die Konzentration des öffentlichen Prozesses im unteren Bereich des Dreiecks. Der linke Sektor zeigt die Konzentration staatlicher Einflussnahme im oberen Bereich. Larry Silverstein ist Teil des nicht-staatlichen Bereichs, aber nicht Teil des öffentlichen Prozesses. Die Pole Politik/Wirtschaft und Medien/öffentliche Meinung als abstrakte Größen bilden ein weiteres Kräftefeld.

Durch die Spiegelung des linken Bereichs erhält man ein auf der Spitze stehendes Dreieck, das die polarisierte Verteilung der Einflussmächte zwischen staatlich institutionell und zivil öffentlich repräsentiert. Ein aus der Betrachtung der Grafik (**fig. 10**, S. 44/45) reduziertes Schema ließe sich nutzen, um diesem grundlegenden Verhältnis nachzugehen. Wo und wie berühren sich die Dreiecke? Lässt sich so ein genereller Unterschied zwischen den politischen Systemen der USA und europäischen Staaten formulieren?

kritik

Wenn auch die Suche nach der Darstellbarkeit der Verhältnisse in diesem Prozess unbefriedigend bleibt, so lassen sich doch Tendenzen bestimmen: Es lassen sich die prinzipiellen Unterschiede in den Strukturen des Gemeinwesens konstatieren. Die Verteilung gesellschaftlicher Aufgaben in den Vereinigten Staaten bemisst die Eigenverantwortung des Individuums mit einem größeren Beitrag als in europäischen Systemen. Dabei kommt es häufig vor, dass Entscheidungsstrukturen nicht von oben nach unten, sondern von unten nach oben gegliedert sind.

Dieser Aspekt des politischen Systems der USA lässt sich mit einem Vergleich aus der Stadtplanung New Yorks illustrieren: Die Konzeption eines regelmäßigen Straßenrasters als Rahmengesetz einer nicht restriktiven, gleichberechtigten und grenzenlosen Entwicklung. Die Vorgabe einer minimalen, gesellschaftlich *guten* und umfassenden Konsenslösung und die Verpflichtung des Einzelnen seinen Teil dazu beizutragen, entsprechen den Beobachtungen, die ich in diesem Prozess gemacht habe.

Anhand dieser Diskussion ließe sich zu der Übertragbarkeit und Vergleichbarkeit für kommunale Planungsprozesse in Deutschland übergehen. In welchen Relationen könnte der New Yorker Prozess ein Vorbild sein oder wie weit reicht die Exzeptionalität der Situation, in der er stattfindet? Hierauf lässt sich keine einfache Antwort finden. Die Vorgänge bis zu diesem Zeitpunkt sind unter besonderen Voraussetzungen motiviert. Der 11. September hat eine Stadt in eine Art Kriegszustand versetzt, nach der physischen Zerstörung und dem insgesamt wirtschaftlichen Nachbeben waren alle Bürger Betroffene: Das kollektive Bewusstsein war derart gerichtet auf die Reparation. Das Wissen um den enormen finanziellen

2002 wurden mit den Bauarbeiten für den Wiederaufbau des Gebäudes 7 WTC und der Rekonstruktion der Haltestellen und Tunnel der U-Bahnen und PATH-Trains begonnen. Außerdem starteten die Port Authority und die LMDC den offiziellen Aufruf zur Einreichung von stadtplanerischen Konzepten für das WTC. In einem auf New York beschränkten Wettbewerb mit 13 Teilnehmern, wurde das Architekturbüro Beyer Blinder Belle Architects & Planners LLP ausgewählt, den ersten Masterplan für das Gelände zu entwickeln. Der Wettbewerb ist Teil eines Zeitplans, den die Port Authority Ende April aufgestellt hat. Die zweite Phase markiert den Auftritt der Institutionen und administrativen Autoritäten als aktive Teilnehmer. Mit ihrem Zeitplan unterstreicht die Port Authority ihre Vorherrschaft in dem Planungsprozess und gerät dabei in die Kritik, die vorherigen Bemühungen und die Kooperation der vielen Beteiligten zu konterkarieren.

Obwohl auf der Veranstaltung *Listening to the City II* die in diesem Wettbewerb vorgelegten Entwürfe von einer breiten Öffentlichkeit vernichtend abgeurteilt wurden, ist in Zukunft ist damit zu rechnen, dass die Aufgabenverteilung stärker durch die Aktion der Institutionen und die Reaktion der Öffentlichkeit als durch ein gemeinsames Vorgehen geprägt sein wird.

wtc und lower manhattan

Um den vielen Unsicherheiten, die sich in der Betrachtung dieses Problemes ergeben haben, zu begegnen, muss als erstes zwischen zwei räumlichen Zonen unterschieden werden, deren Differenz häufig vernachlässigt wird: Lower Manhattan und das Gelände des World Trade Centers. Einerseits ein Stadtteil, und andererseits ein Gebäudekomplex, dessen Dominanz über diesen Stadtteil weit hinaus reicht. Die Zu-

kunft liegt in gegenseitiger Abhängigkeit. Das Zentrum braucht die Umgebung, die Umgebung braucht das Zentrum. Zwar war das WTC wie ein eigener Stadtteil, doch seine Infrastruktur versorgte auch Lower Manhattan – Transport, Nachrichtentechnik, Energie etc. – und umgekehrt (**fig. 4**, S. 37).

Aufgrund der Wechselwirkungen und durch die gemeinsame Ursache verknüpft, denken viele Beteiligte beide Aufgaben gleichzeitig und favorisieren ein Gesamtkonzept vor möglichen Einzellösungen. Doch dazu divergieren die Strukturen der Verantwortung für den einen und den anderen Bereich zu stark.

Die Zukunft des WTC ist abhängig von dem Konsens zwischen vier Parteien: der Port Authority als Eigentümerin, dem Pächter Larry Silverstein, der Lower Manhattan Development Corporation und der Öffentlichkeit (**fig. 5**, S. 36). Hinter der Port Authority (PA) und LMDC stehen der Staat New York und Gouverneur Pataki. Diese Fraktion stellt unzweifelhaft den machtvollsten Part dar. Trotzdem gibt es auch unter diesen beiden erhebliche Unsicherheiten bezüglich ihrer Kompetenzen. Im April 2002 hat man sich darauf geeinigt, dass die Port Authority die Verantwortungen für die Planungen eines neuen WTC verstärken wird, während die LMDC die Koordination des Prozesses für Lower Manhattan, die öffentliche Partizipation, sowie die Erarbeitung eines Zeitrahmens für die Konstituierung eines Mahnmals übernimmt. Entgegen der allgemeinen Annahme, die Entscheidungen lägen in der Hand des Immobilienentwicklers Silverstein, wird sich die Port Authority um die Vergabe von Planungsleistungen bemühen.

Die Dimension, mit der sich der öffentliche Prozess in die Vorstellungen und Rahmenbedingungen des Entwurfs einbringen wird, ist schwer

strukturen

Von Anfang an war die Frage der Macht ein zentrales Thema jeder Diskussion. Es ist bezeichnend, dass bis heute, Juli 2002, keine definitive Antwort möglich ist. Obwohl sich Tendenzen feststellen lassen, die sich im Laufe der Betrachtung verdichtet haben, bleibt der Prozess offen gegen sich verändernde Meinungsbilder und die Beeinflussung durch Medien und Politik. Dabei ist zu beobachten, dass jeweils bestimmte zeitliche Ereignisse die Aufmerksamkeit und öffentliche Wahrnehmung in der Frage der Distribution der Macht auf sich gezogen haben:

Im September 2001 dachten viele, dass Larry Silverstein der Eigentümer sei, und dass er zusammen mit Rudolph Giuliani die Türme als identische Kopie wieder aufbauen wolle.

Im Oktober versprach die Bush-Administration in Washington, den Wiederaufbau von New York mit 20 Milliarden Dollar zu unterstützen.

Im November konnte man meinen, dass die LMDC, die vom Staat und der Stadt New York gegründet worden war, den Wiederaufbau bestimmen würde.

Im Dezember stellte sich Bürgermeister Rudi Giuliani auf die Seite der Familien der Opfer, die forderten, dass die gesamte Fläche einem Friedhof gewidmet würde.

Aber im Januar 2002 trat Mike Bloomberg die Nachfolge von Bürgermeister Giuliani an.

Im Februar hielt die Civic Alliance ihre erste große Konferenz mit 600 Teilnehmern ab, und NewYorkNewVisions und die NYC Partnership veröffentlichten ihre ersten Berichte.

Im März wurde die Kommission der LMDC erweitert, sodass New York City und New York State über gleich viele Posten verfügen. LMDC veröffentlichte ihre Prinzipien für den Wiederaufbau.

Im April haben sich die LMDC und die Port Authority auf eine Verteilung der Aufgaben geeinigt und zur Abgabe von Entwürfen aufgerufen. Die Port Authority hat klargemacht, dass sie diejenige ist, die das Sagen über die Zukunft des Geländes hat.

Diese Veränderungen sind also nur scheinbare Veränderungen, und doch sind sie mehr als nur nominell. In jeder Phase legt sich über das Gerüst der Verantwortlichkeiten eine neue Oberfläche. So bleibt zum Beispiel abzuwarten, was passiert, wenn das Mahnmal zu einer nationalen Gedenkstätte werden sollte und Washington als verantwortlicher Eigentümer auf den Plan tritt.

die phasen

Die erste Phase des Wiederaufbaus war einerseits gekennzeichnet durch die Nachwirkungen des Ereignisses und die direkte Beseitigung der Schäden, sowie andererseits durch den einsetzenden Diskurs. Bevor es zu neuen Planungen kommen konnte, hat in New York eine intensive Wertediskussion über Konzeptionen stattgefunden, die kontemporäre Prinzipien der Stadtentwicklung darstellen könnten. Die Ergebnisse der öffentlichen Kooperation wurden in die Prinzipien der behördlichen und wirtschaftlichen Autoritäten übernommen. Diese Prinzipien stellen einen minimalen Konsens dar, der jedoch viele kontroverse Positionen für weitere Diskussionen offenlässt.

Die zweite Phase wird markiert durch das Ende der Bergungs- und Aufräumarbeiten. Im Mai

Im Juli haben die Lower Manhattan Development Corporation und die Civic Alliance die größte öffentliche Bürgerversammlung zur Zukunft des WTC Geländes ausgerichtet: *Listening to the City II*. Mehr als 5.000 Teilnehmer waren anwesend und haben ihre Vorstellungen, sowie die wenige Tage zuvor erschienen Konzepte des Büros Beyer, Blinder & Belle diskutiert. Die Veranstaltung wurde von *America Speaks* mit einem System elektronischer Datenregistrierung gesponsort, sodass sich augenblicklich Abstimmungsergebnisse ermitteln ließen.

prinzipien newyorknewvisions

1. Ein offener Gedenkprozess
Einen öffentlichen und transparenten Prozess schaffen, um Möglichkeiten und Natur von Gedenkorten und Mahnmalen zu diskutieren und zu organisieren.

2. Eine flexible Mischnutzung von Lower Manhatten
Ansiedlung und Unterstützung verschiedener Nutzungsarten, die sowohl die kulturellen und historischen Aspekte, als auch Handel und Gewerbe berücksichtigt. Schaffung von Büroflächen und einer lebendigen 24-hour-Community.

3. Bessere Verbindung und Anbindung von Downtown Manhattan
Ausbau des öffentlichen Nah- und Fernverkehrs, Bau eines zentralen Verkehrsknotenpunkts: Grand Central Station Downtown, sowie die teilweise Wiedereinführung des alten Straßenrasters und die Überbauung von West Street.

4. Verbesserte Einbindung von Lower Manhatten in der Region
Entwicklung einer Perspektive, die den wachsenden ökonomischen Herausforderungen zwischen Manhattan, Long Island und New Jersey gerecht wird.

5. Vorbildliche Gestaltung und Nachhaltige Entwürfe
Design, Architektur und Gestaltung mit einem Schwerpunkt auf der nachhaltigen Entwicklung von New York City.

6. Die Einhaltung eines umfassenden öffentlichen Prozesses
Entwicklung eines umfassenden Plans für Lower Manhattan mit lang- und kurzfristigen Strategien für die Stadt- und Raumplanung. Der Prozess soll durch die Beteiligung des administrativen, des privaten und des öffentlichen Sektors ausgeführt werden.

7. Sofortige Aktionen
Die Möglichkeit temporärer Gedenkorte schaffen, auf die Bedürfnisse der Bewohner achten, den öffentlichen Nahverkehr so schnell wie möglich wiederherstellen und Hilfe für Kleingewerbe bereitstellen.

(NYNV Report, Februar 2002)

zu formulieren. Sie arbeitet eng mit der LMDC, der Port Authority und der New York City Planning Commission zusammen. Die Regional Planning Association (RPA) und eine Gruppe akademischer Partner, wie die New York University, die New School University und das Pratt Institute PICCED, stellen Personal und andere Ressourcen bereit. Die Civic Alliance verfügt über eine ebenso große und komplexe Struktur von Arbeitsgruppen und Mitarbeitern wie die LMDC. Es sind oft dieselben Personen, die in beiden Organisationen vertreten sind. Diese Doppelungen treten auch in der Civic Alliance und ihren Gründungsvereinen auf, wie zum Beispiel NewYorkNewVisions.

Die am 11. März für 31 Tage eröffnete Lichtinstallation *Tribute in Light* (ursprünglich *Towers of Light*) ist auch ein Projekt, das auf Privatinitiative entstanden ist und durch das Engagement und die Unterstützung nicht-staatlicher Organisationen verwirklicht werden konnte. Wenige Tage nach dem 11. September erschienen zwei unabhängige, aber ähnliche Vorschläge für eine Lichtskulptur aus zwei Lichtstrahlen, die an die Türme des WTC erinnern sollten. Unter der Vermittlung der Municipal Art Society schlossen sich die Künstler und Architekten zu einem Team zusammen. Die Idee gewann sehr schnell allgemeine Anerkennung und wurde bis zur Realisierung zu einem Allgemeingut. „It's nice! The lights are cool!", war die allgemein zu vernehmende Resonanz als die Lichttürme am 11. März zum ersten Mal kilometerweit in den Himmel ragten. Neben dem Bekenntnis zu dem temporären Charakter gab es viele Meinungen, die das erneute Verschwinden der Türme bedauerten.

Im März wurde über die Umzäunung des Geländes während der Fundamentierungsarbeiten und der Rekonstruktion der U-Bahn Tunnel und Stationen diskutiert. Nachdem der Chef der Port Authority einen zehn Meter hohen Holzwall vorgeschlagen hatte, um die Öffentlichkeit vor dem Anblick der Baustelle zu schützen, schlug ihm eine Welle des allgemeinen Protestes entgegen, sodass er sich gezwungen sah, sich mit einer anderen Konzeption auseinanderzusetzen. In einer nicht öffentlichen Sitzung mit verschiedenen Teilnehmern privater Planungsinitiativen, unter anderem NYNV, wurde dann ein Zaun entworfen, der die Bedeutung des Ortes für die Bevölkerung nicht negiert, sondern als durchlässige Umhüllung gestaltet, die den verschiedenen Bedürfnissen des Gedenkens und der Anteilnahme Rechnung trägt.

Im April veranstaltete die *Municipal Art Society* zusammen mit der New York University, der New School University und dem Pratt Institute Center for Community and Environmental Development, ihre Workshop Serie *Imagine New York*. Über hundert Seminare wurden in allen Stadtteilen New Yorks, sowie in New Jersey und Connecticut ausgerichtet. Ihr Ziel war es, das Stimmungsbild der Allgemeinheit nachzuzeichnen, um so eine Grundlage für eine allseits anerkannte Planung herzustellen. Drei Fragen waren zu beantworten: „Was haben wir verloren und wie haben wir uns verändert? Wie sollte die Zukunft aussehen? Welche übergeordneten Themen lassen sich daraus ableiten?"
(**fig. 13**, S. 50/51)

Über 2.000 Menschen haben an diesen Veranstaltungen teilgenommen. Die ungeheure Fülle des Datenmaterials wurde im Nachgang sortiert, gefiltert und statistisch aufbereitet. Im Juli wurden die Ergebnisse präsentiert. Sie zeichnen dabei ein erstaunlich konsistentes Meinungsbild, da sich in den unterschiedlichen Nachbarschaften dieselben übergeordneten Prinzipien widerspiegelten.

sis öffentlicher Akzeptanz einzutreten. In sieben Arbeitsgruppen widmet man sich Themen wie Transport, Infrastruktur, Kultur, Stadtplanung, Gedenkprozess.

Die Arbeitsgruppe *Memorial Process* hat bereits im November zu Gesprächsrunden eingeladen, bei denen Betroffene und Vertreter unterschiedlicher Interessensgruppen zu den Möglichkeiten des Gedenkens und der Errichtung eines Mahnmals Stellung bezogen haben (Familienangehörige von Opfern, Bergungskräfte, Bewohner, Immobilienbesitzer, Kaufleute, führende Wirtschaftsunternehmen u.a.).

Die Arbeitsgruppe *Temporary Memorials* hat sehr viel dazu beigetragen, den Prozess noch stärker in das Blickfeld der Debatte um das Ermahnen und Gedenken zu rücken, und damit die Komponente der Zeit gegen den Anspruch der Dauerhaftigkeit einzuführen. Zum Beispiel publizierte sie eine Reihe periodisch erscheinender Karten, die zeigen, wie sich die Situation des Unglücksortes, der Zustand umliegender Bebauung und die Trauer- und Gedächtniswände verändert haben.

Im Dezember haben NYNV bereits einen Report mit Prinzipien für den Wiederaufbau von Lower Manhattan vorgelegt. Dieses Heft wurde als das erste bedeutende stadtplanerische Konzept nach der Einführung des Straßenrasters 1811 begrüßt. Die hier erarbeiteten Grundzüge sind fast unverändert in den offiziellen Entwurf, den die Lower Manhattan Development Corporation im April vorgestellt hat, übernommen worden.

Am 15. November hat die New York City Partnership, ein spontaner Zusammenschluss führender Unternehmensberater (McKinsey, KPMG u.a.), ihren ersten Bericht über die ökonomischen Folgen des 11. Septembers für die New Yorker Wirtschaft vorgestellt. Eine auf Eigeninitiative und -interesse verfasste Studie, die sehr genau über den Zustand der betroffenen Branchen Auskunft und Anweisungen für einen schnellen Wiederaufbau gibt.

Unzufrieden mit dem Stand der Diskussionen um die Wiederbebauung des WTC Geländes hatte der New Yorker Galerist Max Protetch die Idee zu der Ausstellung *A New World Trade Center*. Im Januar eröffnete er die umstrittene, doch erfolgreiche Ausstellung mit 35 ambitionierten Entwürfen und Ideen international namhafter Architekten für ein neues World Trade Center. Kritik entfiel auf die Haltung, mit der anmaßenden Souveränität des entwerfenden Individuums die Situation künstlerhaft zu trivialisieren.

Ebenfalls im Januar eröffnete Exit Art die Ausstellung *Reactions*. Auf eine Ausschreibung, was der 11. September bedeute und wie er das Leben oder die Sichtweise verändert habe, erhielt Exit Art ca. 10.000 internationale Beiträge. Die Antworten auf Blättern im US-Letter-Format sind alle in den Galerieräumen ausgestellt.

Die *Civic Alliance to Rebuild Downtown New York* hat am 7. Februar die erste große öffentliche Anhörung veranstaltet. Zu ihrem *Listening to the City* kamen ca. 600 Menschen zusammen, die ihre Bedenken, Sorgen, Anregungen und Wünsche für den Prozess und die anstehenden Aufgaben vor Verantwortlichen privater und staatlicher Institutionen vorgetragen haben.

Die Civic Alliance versteht sich als eine Art Schirmgesellschaft der vielfältigen privaten, öffentlichen Planungsambitionen. Über 100 Wirtschaftsverbände, Bürgervereine, Umwelt- und Planungsgruppen haben sich hier zusammengeschlossen, um eine gemeinsame Vision für die Zukunft von Ground Zero und Lower Manhattan

der öffentliche prozess

Das Zusammenwirken der verschiedenen privaten, öffentlichen, bürgerlichen, sozialen und zivilen Initiativen bezeichne ich als *öffentlichen Prozess* (Public Process).

Der öffentliche Prozess zeigt zum einen das Stimmungsbild der Allgemeinheit, zum anderen vermag er Ideen, Energien und Kreativität freizusetzen, die über die institutionellen und administrativen Ressourcen hinausreichen. Er ist ein Korrektiv in der Entscheidungsgewalt und der Ideenfindung. Das Prinzip der öffentlichen Partizipation ist zudem ein Grundprinzip angewandter Demokratie.

Der öffentliche Prozess findet auf verschiedenen Ebenen statt: Er wird konkret sichtbar in den unorganisierten, unkontrollierten Meinungsäußerungen, wie sie sich in den spontanen Mahnmalen, Lichterprozessionen, den Schreinen und Erinnerungstableaus ausdrücken. In Umfragen, Workshops und öffentlichen Veranstaltungen wird auf der Grundlage soziologischer und statistischer Strukturen versucht, ein konkret messbares Bild der öffentlichen Meinung zu gewinnen. Und drittens lässt sich die Selbstorganisation der Zivilgesellschaft in privaten und öffentlichen Vereinigungen und Interessensverbände beobachten.

Um gesellschaftliche, wirtschaftliche oder politische Verantwortung zu übernehmen, ist es entscheidend, dass diese Gruppen auf bestehende Kommunikationsstrukturen und gut funktionierende Lobbyarbeit zurück greifen können. Das Internet gewinnt als Multiplikator der globalen Vernetzung und des Informationsaustausches eine starke Bedeutung für die Open-Source-Bewegung öffentlicher Prozesse.

Am Anfang aller öffentlichen Partizipation stehen die vielen über die Stadt verteilten spontanen Mahnmale, die zum Teil immer noch erneuert und gepflegt werden. Die *Missing* Blätter sind zu einer eigenen Kunstform avanciert (**img. 2-7**, **S. 33**). Als Zweites sind die vielen Vorschläge, Ideen und Entwürfe zu nennen, die zu Tausenden die verschiedenen Institutionen und Initiativen erreichen, und deren Quantität die bestehenden Kapazitäten übersteigt, weshalb es verschiedene Initiativen gibt, die sich der Verwaltung dieser Beiträge annehmen.

Die erste Initiative zur öffentlichen Partizipation war die Ausstellung *Here is New York. A Democracy of Photographs*, die Anfang Oktober eröffnet wurde. Das Anliegen der Initiatoren war es, durch die Archivierung des fotografischen Materials, die Einzelerfahrung der Allgemeinheit zugänglich zu machen und einen kollektiven Pool der fotografischen Erinnerung anzulegen. Dabei wurde ausdrücklich auf die Unterscheidung zwischen Aufnahmen von Professionellen und Amateuren verzichtet. Die abgegebenen Fotos wurden digitalisiert und archiviert. Sie werden in den Galerieräumen ausgestellt und können als A3-Ausdrucke erworben werden. Der Erlös von $ 25 pro Ausdruck geht an eine Initiative für die Kinder der Verstorbenen. Seit der Eröffnung im Oktober ist der Ansturm der Besucher kaum geringer geworden. *Here is New York* wurde seitdem auch in anderen Städten der Welt fortgesetzt. Im August 2002 war die Ausstellung im Berliner Martin-Gropius-Bau zu sehen.

Die Koalition NewYorkNewVisions hatte sich bereits wenige Tage nach dem 11. September zusammengeschlossen, um gemeinsam Strategien für New York, Manhattan, Ground Zero und den gesamten Planungs- und Denkprozess zu untersuchen. Ein Grundsatz ist die Verpflichtung, für einen umfassenden, offenen Prozess auf der Bader Bundesstaaten New York und New Jersey. Interessen von Öffentlichkeit, Regierung und Privatwirtschaft treffen aufeinander. Zugleich hat sich die wachsende Organisation von Meinungs- und Interessensverbänden als gleichstarker Gesprächspartner für die Zukunft von Lower Manhattan und das Gelände des WTC etabliert.

Da die Auswirkungen des 11. Septembers so umfassend die Funktionen der Stadt ergriffen haben, ist Silverstein wie alle anderen auf die Revitalisierung der Stadt angewiesen. Für das entsprechende Entwicklungsprogramm hat Washington 20 Milliarden Dollar zugesagt. Nur von dem konjunkturellen Aufschwung kann sich Silverstein profitablen Umsatz aus der Vermietung seines neuen WTC erhoffen. Es wäre unklug, sich nicht entsprechend kooperativ zu verhalten.

New York State Governor George E. Pataki

Gouverneur Pataki gilt als die einflussreichste Person bei den Planungen für das Gelände des WTC (**fig. 11**, S.46/47). Von den 14 Mitgliedern des Vorstandes der LMDC hat er sieben einberufen, darunter den Posten des Vorsitzenden, John C. Whitehead, und das Amt des Präsidenten und ausführenden Direktors, Louis Tomson. Die LMDC ist eine Division der ESDC, deren Vorsitz Charles Gargano führt, ein enger Mitarbeiter und Vertrauter Patakis. Außerdem kontrolliert Gouverneur Pataki die Port Authority, zusammen mit dem noch etwas unerfahrenen und wenig profilierten Gouverneur McGreedy von New Jersey. Er hat sechs der zwölf Vorstandsmitglieder gewählt, zusätzlich wird der Posten des Vizepräsidenten von seinem Bekannten, Gargano, bestritten.

Pataki befindet sich bereits im Wahlkampf für die im November 2002 anstehenden Wahlen zum Amt des Gouverneurs von New York. Sein möglicher demokratischer Herausforderer Andrew Cuomo hat ihm in letzter Zeit medienwirksam vorgeworfen, die Entwicklung von Ground Zero würde zu langsam vorangehen. Sein Erfolg bei der Wiederwahl wird von der öffentlichen Wahrnehmung seiner Leistung in diesem Prozess abhängen.

NYC Mayor Mike Bloomberg

Im Dezember 2001 wurde Bloomberg als Nachfolger von Rudolph Giuliani zum Bürgermeister von New York gewählt. Giuliani hatte sich als Mann der „Zero Tolerance" bei der öffentlichen Sicherheit und als tröstender, standhafter Krisenmanager nach dem 11. September profiliert.

Bloomberg, der sich nicht als Politiker, sondern als Manager versteht, steht vor der schwierigen Aufgabe, den wirtschaftlichen Wiederaufbau, negative Haushaltsbilanzen und die Arbeitslosigkeit in den Griff zu bekommen. Seine Rolle beim Wiederaufbau des World Trade Centers ist dennoch eher ideel, da er nur über geringe Mittel der Einflussnahme verfügt.

Community Boards

Community Boards sind unabhängige Organisationen von Bewohnern lokal begrenzter Gebiete. Seit den Grass Roots/Civil Rights Bewegungen der 1960er-Jahre hat ihre Bedeutung und politische Einflussnahme stark zugenommen. Sie stehen in enger Kooperation mit kommunalpolitischen Institutionen. Kein Projekt kann ohne vorherige Präsentation, Diskussion und Billigung der Community Boards verwirklicht werden.

In Lower Manhattan leben ca. 20.000 Menschen. Das WTC Grundstück liegt auf der Grenze von CB#1 und #2.

New York mit New Jersey verbinden. Sie betreibt außerdem zwei Subway Linien, die PATH trains (Port Authority Trans Hudson), die unterhalb des Hudson River zwischen Jersey City und Manhattan verkehren. Auf dem Grundstück des WTC befindet sich einer der vier Knotenpunkte des PATH-Systems, den täglich 50.000 Pendler auf ihrem Weg zur Arbeit in Downtown benutzten.

Die Port Authority ist in ihrer Funktion als Eigentümerin eine der entscheidenden Figuren in der Frage um die Zukunft am Ground Zero.

Larry Silverstein Consortium

Erst Ende Juli 2001 hatte Larry Silverstein die sechs Gebäude des World Trade Centers für 99 Jahre von der Port Authority gepachtet, sechs Wochen vor dem 11. September.

Das Gebäude 7 WTC – ebenfalls Port Authority, und nördlich der Plaza gelegen – hatte er bereits in den achtziger Jahren gepachtet. Es kollabierte am 11. September gegen 18 Uhr Ortszeit aufgrund der Beschädigungen durch den Einsturz des Nordturmes. Seit der Zerstörung strebte Silverstein an, einen Neubau auf demselben Grundriss zu errichten. Nach starken Protesten der Öffentlichkeit gegen sein Vorhaben, ein Gebäude in den Abmessungen des Vorgängerbaus zu errichten, da dieses dem Kriterium der Wiedereinführung des Straßenrasters, nämlich der Durchführung von Greenwich Street widersprochen hätte, erklärte er sich bereit, den Neubau auf eine Seite der Straße zu beschränken und auf 20 % Bürofläche zu verzichten. Die Bauarbeiten zu einem neuen 7 WTC haben im Mai begonnen.

Gründe dafür, warum Silverstein bei der Planung dieser Immobilie relativ freie Hand gelassen wurde, könnten sein: unterschiedliche vertragliche Verpflichtungen, die räumliche Distanz, Zugeständnisse an den Umsatz seines Unternehmens, sowie die Notwendigkeit, die zehn Transformatoren der ConEdison zu ersetzen und damit die Stromversorgung von Lower Manhattan zu konsolidieren. In Bezug auf das Gelände des WTC sind seine Zugriffsmöglichkeiten allerdings stark begrenzt. Hierfür lassen sich vier Gründe anführen: der Streit um die Versicherungsprämie, die komplexe Eigentums- und Interessenlage, die Abhängigkeit von der wirtschaftlichen Entwicklung und der Zeitfaktor.

Momentan befindet sich das Silverstein Consortium in einem Rechtsstreit mit den Versicherungsträgern über die Höhe der Versicherungssumme. Silverstein behauptet, dass es sich um zwei Ereignisse handelt, zwei Flugzeuge, zwei Anschläge. Die Versicherung argumentiert, dass es sich um einen Terroranschlag mit zwei Flugzeugen handelt. Je nachdem wie die Bundesrichter entscheiden, erhält Silverstein die einfache oder doppelte Versicherungssumme für den Schadensfall (3,5 Milliarden Dollar). Der Ausgang dieses Verfahrens ist von einiger Brisanz, denn sollte das Gericht für die Version der unabhängigen Ereignisse votieren, wäre mit politischen Implikationen von größerem Ausmaß zu rechnen.

Nach den ersten Reaktionen, die einen originalgetreuen Wiederaufbau forderten, trat Silverstein mit seiner Variante von vier identischen aber halb so hohen Gebäuden an die Öffentlichkeit. Für viele ein Zeichen dafür, dass auch diesmal die Entscheidungsgewalt in den Händen einzelner mächtiger Personen läge. Unterdessen ist die Situation eine andere, denn als Pächter ist Silverstein an die vertraglichen Pflichten gegenüber der Port Authority gebunden. Die staatliche Gesellschaft untersteht den Gouverneuren

Die folgende Aufzählung nennt Personen, Gruppen und Institutionen, die in direkter Verbindung mit den Diskussionen um den Wiederaufbau von Lower Manhattan stehen und von denen die Hälfte nach dem 11. September entstanden sind:

September's Mission – Rebuilding with a Spotlight on the Poor, SPOT – Wallstreetrising – Widows and Families 911 – Rebuild Downtown Our Town, R.DoT – Regional Planning Association, RPA – Families of September 11 – Give Your Voice WTC – New York State Governor Pataki – Ground Zero Task Force – Labor Community Advocacy Network – Larry Silverstein Consortium – Lower Manhattan Development Corporation, LMDC – Civic Alliance to Rebuild Lower Manhattan – NYC Partnership – New York New Visions, NYNV – Community Boards No. 1, 2, 3 – Downtown Alliance – Municipal Art Society, MAS – NYC Rebuild – City Council's Select Committee on Lower Manhattan Redevelopment – City Planning Commission – Empire State Transportation Alliance – Mayor Bloomberg – Mass Transportation Authority, MTA – Office of Regional and Community Affairs of the Federal Reserve Bank of New York, ORCA – Port Authority New York New Jersey, PANYNJ – Real Estate Board of New York

distributionen der macht

Lower Manhattan Development Corporation

Die LMDC ist eine Tochter der Empire State Development Corporation New York, ESDC. Sie untersteht den Weisungen des Gouverneurs. Die staatliche Gesellschaft wurde im Herbst 2001 von Gouverneur George E. Pataki und Bürgermeister Rudolph Giuliani eingesetzt, um die Verantwortung für die Entwicklung und den Wiederaufbau des World Trade Centers und Lower Manhattan zu übernehmen. Sieben Mitglieder der Kommission wurden von Pataki, und vier von Giuliani berufen. Ihre Provenienz ist durchweg aus den höheren Kreisen des „Big Business" mit entsprechenden Verbindungen zur Politik. Da Bürgermeister Bloomberg bisher kein Mitspracherecht in den Planungen hatte, wurde die Kommission im März um weitere drei von ihm zu benennende Mitglieder erweitert.

Die LMDC hat im März Alexander Garvin als vorsitzenden Stadtplaner ins Amt berufen. Desweiteren hat man mehrere Arbeitsgruppen gebildet, die sich mit den unterschiedlichen Themengebieten befassen werden. Die komplizierte Struktur der Gesellschaft gleicht inzwischen der einer Behörde.

Zu den wichtigsten Inhalten und Aufgaben zählen Supervision, Kontakt zur Öffentlichkeit, Koordination mit Stadt, Staat und Washington, sowie die Verteilung der 20 Milliarden Dollar aus Washington. Die LMDC gilt als die entscheidende Schnittstelle zwischen den beteiligten Institutionen, Entscheidungsträgern und der Öffentlichkeit.

Port Authority of New York & New Jersey

Die PANYNJ ist die Eigentümerin des Grundstückes und war bis 2001 auch Betreiberin des World Trade Centers, das sie erst Ende Juli 2001 für 99 Jahre an Larry Silverstein verpachtet hat.

Die Port Authority ist eine Gesellschaft, die je zur Hälfte den beiden Staaten New York und New Jersey gehört. Es ist die einzige bistaatliche Organisation der USA. In ihrem Besitz befinden sich die drei Großflughäfen John F. Kennedy, La Guardia und Newark, sowie alle Brücken und Tunnel, die die Inseln von New York, sowie

an die Hinterbliebenen zur Abgabe von DNA enthaltenden persönlichen Gegenständen folgte im März 2002 ein weiterer, da das abgegebene Material für eine DNA Analyse zur Identifikation der Opfer nicht ausreichend war. Von den 2.825 Toten sind bisher ungefähr ein Drittel identifiziert worden.

Überlegungen stehen an, wie mit den 19.132 Knochen und anderen nicht identifizierbaren Überresten verfahren werden soll. Wahrscheinlich werden sie bis zu einem späteren Zeitpunkt, wenn verbesserte Analysetechniken vorliegen, in einem Grab der unbekannten Opfer des 11. Septembers beigelegt. Bis dahin werden sie in dreißig Tiefkühlcontainern an der 30. Straße aufbewahrt.

Es wurden vielfältige Fonds für die Opfer des 11. Septembers eingerichtet, wie beispielsweise für Hinterbliebene von Feuerwehrleuten, Polizeibeamten und Firmenangestellten, sowie für die Ausbildung ihrer Kinder, für die Bewohner von Lower Manhattan, für kleine Wirtschaftsbetriebe, Selbstständige, Künstler und Designer.

der prozess

Der Wiederaufbau von Lower Manhattan gilt als das größte Projekt in den Vereinigten Staaten in den nächsten Jahren. Und dieses Projekt wird von einem eben so großen öffentlichen Interesse begleitet. Die Öffentlichkeit verlangt, dass dieser Prozess umfassend und transparent für alle Betroffenen und Beteiligten ist, und dass er zum Prinzip einer gemeinsamen Suche nach der Zukunft gemacht wird.

Die Erstellung einer Generalplanung mit so vielfältigen Implikationen ist kein einfaches Unterfangen. Es ist ein langwieriger Prozess. Nicht nur deswegen, weil in den Zentren der größten Wirtschaftsnationen, Großprojekte ein langes und kompliziertes Genehmigungsverfahren auf allen Ebenen zu durchlaufen haben.

Nach dem 11. September haben sich schätzungsweise einige Hundert Gruppen und Initiativen zusammengefunden, um direkte Aufgaben und Probleme anzugehen, und sich mit den aufkommenden Fragen zu beschäftigen. Einige von ihnen waren von nur begrenzter Dauer, andere haben ihre Ziele auf zukünftige Planung und Mitgestaltung erweitert. Wenn man davon ausgeht, dass vielleicht vierzig Gruppen aktiv sind, und jede davon aus Mitgliedern von ca. 30 anderen bereits bestehenden Institutionen und Organisationen gegründet wurde (z. B. NYNV: 22, NYC Partnership: 40, Civic Alliance: 100), erhält man eine Zahl von ca. 1.200 Gruppierungen, die in den Wiederaufbau von Lower Manhattan involviert sind. Dieses Rechenbeispiel verdeutlicht die Dimension des Vorgangs. Absolute Zahlen sind schwer zu beziffern, weil viele Personen in mehreren Gruppen gleichzeitig aktiv sind und Hochschulen und Universitäten als wissenschaftliche Ressourcen und Hauptsponsor mehrerer Initiativen fungieren.

frastruktur und einen günstigeren Grundstückspreis bieten können.

Die Katastrophe des 11. Septembers hat nahezu alle Tendenzen der wirtschaftlichen Umstrukturierung katalytisch beschleunigt: sowohl die Rezession, das Fallen der Aktienkurse nach der geplatzten Dotcom-Blase, den Niedergang des Arbeitsmarktes, wie auch die Dezentralisierung in der betrieblichen Standortpolitik und die daraus folgenden Aufgaben für die Stadtplanung.

von ground zero zu fresh kills

Fresh Kills (von kill = niedl.: Bachlauf) Name einer Region auf Staten Island, die bis Ende 2000 als zentrale Mülldeponie von New York City genutzt wurde.

Ende Mai 2002 sind die Bergungs- und Aufräumarbeiten vollständig abgeschlossen und 1,6 Millionen Tonnen Trümmer und Schutt beseitigt (davon allein 200.000 Tonnen Stahl aus der Konstruktion der Türme). Man ist damit dem aufgestellten Zeitplan um ein halbes Jahr voraus. Für die Beseitigung der Trümmer haben sich Freiwillige aus dem ganzen Land gemeldet. Gearbeitet wird Tag und Nacht. Versorgt werden sie ebenfalls von freiwilligen Helfern, die Unterkunft und Verpflegung stellen.

Eine Flutlichtanlage sorgt neben der notwendigen Beleuchtung für eine bisweilen ätherische Stimmung über der Grube, welche noch immer von der Polizei abgeriegelt ist. Damit möglichst wenig schädlicher Staub bei dem Transport aufgewirbelt wird, werden die Straßen und die ein- und ausfahrenden Lastwagen mit Wasser feucht gehalten.

Während sich die giftigen Staubablagerungen auf den Fassaden und in den Straßen durch Winderosion verflüchtigt haben, stellt die Verschmutzung von Privatwohnungen durch den asbest- und schwermetallhaltigen Staub aus den Baumaterialien des World Trade Centers ein nachhaltiges Problem dar: Durch nicht fachgemäße Beseitigung wurden ordnungsgemäß gereinigte Bereiche erneut kontaminiert. Die Risiken für die Gesundheit der Bevölkerung sind hier unkalkulierbar. Erst im Mai 2002 hat das Umweltbundesamt bekannt gegeben, es würde die Reinigung von Privathaushalten übernehmen. Als Folge dieser heraus gezögerten Maßnahme zeichnet sich ab, dass sich einige Bewohner von Downtown mit einer Sammelklage an Washington wenden werden.

Im Mai lassen einige der umliegenden Gebäude noch Beschädigungen durch den Einsturz der Zwillingstürme erkennen. Von den elf geschlossenen Subway Stationen sind seit Dezember bereits acht wieder in Betrieb. Eine Besucherplattform wurde installiert, die Touristen einen eintrittspflichtigen Ausblick ermöglicht. Die Einnahmen fließen in spezielle Fonds für die Hinterbliebenen.

Die Trümmer der sieben Gebäude werden mit Lastwagen zum nahe gelegenen Hudson River gefahren, dort auf Schiffe geladen und zur wieder eröffneten Mülldeponie Fresh Kills gebracht. Teile der Stahlkonstruktion werden zur genauen Untersuchung der Einsturzursache zu einem Salvage Yard nach Newark transportiert.

Die Mülldeponie Fresh Kills gilt als die größte von Menschenhand geschaffene Struktur, und soll wie die Chinesische Mauer vom All aus sichtbar sein. Dort ist ein riesiges Freiluft-Laboratorium entstanden, in dem die Schuttlieferungen des WTC noch einmal nach menschlichen Überresten, Wertgegenständen und Datenträgern durchsucht werden. Einem ersten Aufruf

Das World Trade Center besaß eine eigene Postleitzahl: *New York 10047/48*. Das Grundstück ist ein unregelmäßiges Trapezoid, annähernd quadratisch, und hat eine Größe von sechseinhalb Hektar. Das Grundstück ist Eigentum der *Port Authority of New York & New Jersey* (PANYNJ), einer bistaatlichen Hafen- und Verkehrsgesellschaft, die sämtliche Gebäude des WTC im Juli 2001 für 99 Jahre an das Larry Silverstein Consortium verpachtet hatte.

Das WTC ist als sogenannter „Superblock" über zwölf vorhandene Blöcke geplant worden und hat somit die historischen Straßenverläufe unterbrochen. Die Infrastruktur bestand bis zum 11. September aus einem Kopfbahnhof der PATH Trains (Port Authority Trans Hudson), drei Subway Stationen, zehn Transformatoren der Consolidated Edison in 7 WTC und einer 100 Meter hohen Sendeanlage auf dem Nordturm.

die situation

14 % der Steuereinnahmen und ein Viertel des Wirtschaftsvolumens der Stadt New York erwirtschaftet der Sektor der Finanzdienstleistungen. Von den 370.000 Jobs in Lower Manhattan gehören 49 % in diesen Sektor, der 77 % des Umsatzes in Lower Manhattan bestreitet. Lower Manhattan ist das drittgrößte ökonomische Zentrum in den Vereinigten Staaten, nach Midtown Manhattan und Chicago. Von den 3,7 Millionen Arbeitsplätzen in NYC waren 10% in Lower Manhattan. 1250 Firmen arbeiteten in den sieben Gebäuden des WTC. Nach dem 11. September wurden 100.000 Jobs nach Midtown verlagert oder in anderen Bereichen außerhalb der Stadt untergebracht.

2,3 Millionen m^2 Bürofläche, 30 % von Lower Manhattan, waren zerstört oder unbenutzbar, davon eine Millionen m^2 in dem zerstörten Komplex des WTC, 300.000 m^2 schwer beschädigt und 1 Millionen m^2 konnten nach baldiger Instandsetzung wieder bezogen werden. Von den großen Firmen wie American Express, Morgan Stanley und Goldman Sachs werden viele mit einem Großteil der Angestellten zurückkommen. Doch setzt sich in der Betriebsführung allmählich der Trend zur Dezentralisierung durch, so dass gewisse Ressourcen an verschiedenen Orten verbleiben oder neu installiert werden.

Der wirtschaftliche Schaden des 11. Septembers wird auf 83 Milliarden Dollar geschätzt. Das entspricht fast einem Fünftel (19 %) des Wirtschaftsvolumens der Stadt New York (440 Milliarden Dollar). Abzüglich der Versicherungszahlungen und der staatlichen Zuschüsse bleibt ein vergleichsweise geringes Minus von 16 Milliarden Dollar. In der ganzen Stadt sind seitdem ca. 100.000 Jobs verloren gegangen. Man rechnet damit, dass sich diese Zahl bis Ende 2003 auf 57.000 verringern wird. Die Arbeitslosigkeit ist seit September 2001 von 5 % auf 7,5 % angestiegen.

Große Verluste haben die Tourismusindustrie (25.000 verlorene Jobs), Einzelhandel (Rückgang um 14 %), der Immobilienmarkt (Mieten in Lower Manhattan um 13 % gefallen) und kleinere Dienstleistungsbetriebe (ca. 1.000 Konkurse) erlitten. Der Personenflugverkehr ist um 20% zurückgegangen.

Große Konkurrenz für den Standort NYC bedeutet die Nähe von Jersey City auf der anderen Seite des Hudson River. Hier siedeln sich seit einigen Jahren verstärkt große Unternehmen an, was sich an der rasant wachsenden Skyline nachvollziehen lässt. New York ist deswegen darauf bedacht, so schnell wie möglich Flächen in den fünf Stadtteilen zu attraktiven Wirtschaftsstandorten zu entwickeln, die eine entsprechende In-

ground zero

Ground Zero (deutsch: Bodennullpunkt) bezeichnet die Explosionsstelle einer Bombe, Atombombe oder Rakete über dem Boden; seit dem 11. September 2001 steht der Begriff auch für das zerstörte World Trade Center in New York.

Die Welt versammelt sich vor dem Fernseher. New York versammelt sich auf der Straße. Trotz der globalen Dimension des Ereignisses und weltweit vernetzter Kommunikationssysteme bleibt die Welt nur Zuschauer und ein kleiner Teil wird wirklich zu direkt Betroffenen. Während sich die internationale und nationale Perspektive bald auf andere Themen und Konflikte konzentriert, bleibt die regionale Perspektive an dieses Grundstück geheftet. Und es ist entscheidend für das Verständnis des Prozesses, zu bedenken, dass diese regionale Perspektive die Realität der Ereignisse und der Folgen für diesen Ort bezeugt.

das fundament

Die Aufräumarbeiten bereiten die Grundlage für die Errichtung der Zukunft. Aufräumen bedeutet hier die Bergung von Leichenteilen und die Beseitigung von 1,6 Millionen Tonnen Trümmern. Zurück bleibt ein 20 Meter tiefes Loch mit einer riesigen Betonwanne, aus der alle Reste des Vorherigen herausgekratzt wurden. Die Diskrepanz zwischen der anscheinenden Neutralität des Ortes und seiner historischen Signifikanz ist unbeschreiblich. Eine leere Fläche mitten in der Stadt. Sowohl die Türme, wie auch die Ruinen sind verschwunden. Ähnelt die Szenerie jetzt schon einer Baustelle, so wird sie genau das in den nächsten Jahren bleiben.

Parallel zu der Bereitstellung des Fundaments verläuft die Suche nach der Grundlage zukünftiger Planungen. Die frühen Spekulationen und Ambitionen verstummten, als abzusehen war, dass sich keine einfache Antwort als Reaktion auf die Komplexität der Situation finden lassen würde. Die großen Fragen wurden zurückgestellt und es begann eine Arbeit im Kleinen. Der Prozess entwickelte sich weiter, indem sich eine breite Öffentlichkeit beteiligte und organisierte. Auf der Basis vielfältiger Eigeninitiativen wurde nach einem Weg zum Konsens aller Beteiligten gesucht. Der öffentliche Prozess machte aus der Frage die Antwort. Die Reaktion der Gemeinschaft ersetzt die Reaktion stellvertretend für die Gemeinschaft. Die Frage war nicht „Was", sondern „Wie". Doch damit wurde der Prozess selbst zum Gegenstand der Diskussion.

Die Diskussionen haben gezeigt, dass ein Thema am häufigsten die Gedanken und Gemüter bewegt hat: die Frage nach den Strukturen von Macht, Einfluss und Mitbestimmung in diesem Prozess. Hierauf hat es zu verschiedenen Zeiten verschiedene Antworten gegeben. Erst, wenn das Ergebnis unumstößlich feststeht, wird sich nachvollziehen lassen, wer welchen Anteil hatte. Doch auch dann sollte das Ergebnis nicht mit dem Prozess gleichgesetzt werden.

das grundstück

Das Grundstück des ehemaligen World Trade Centers liegt in Downtown Manhattan, Financial District, in der Nähe der Wallstreet und neben dem World Financial Center, zwischen West Street, Vesey Street, Church Street und Liberty Street. Zwischen dem Grundstück und dem WFC verläuft der West Side Highway südwärts in den Brooklyn Battery Tunnel, eine Hauptverbindung zwischen Manhattan und Brooklyn. Im Osten befinden sich St. Paul's Church and Churchyard.

Gebäude zur Zeit ihrer Errichtung, bis zu den diversen Trump Towers. Dann wäre aber nicht erklärt, warum das World Trade Center sich dennoch als Ziel ausgezeichnet hätte. Das Entscheidende hier ist nicht das Allgemeine (der größte Welthandelspenis der USA steht in Chicago), sondern das Besondere.

Für Symboliker war der 11. September das größte Ereignis überhaupt, ein Krieg der Symbole: Flugzeuge als Symbole, Hochhäuser als Symbole und Bilder als Ikonen. Unter dem Eindruck der Bilder erwuchsen Kommentare wie Baudrillards „symbolische Herausforderung", Lévi-Strauss' „Verlust der metaphysischen Intelligenz" und Stockhausens „Kunstwerk". Symbolisierungen dienen der Aneignung und Instrumentalisierung von Phänomenen. Sie interpretieren und politisieren zugunsten subjektiver Anschauungen und Vorstellungen. Es lässt sich heute kaum noch aufzählen, welche verschiedenen Symbolisierungen das World Trade Center von Anfang bis Ende durchlaufen hat.

Die Meinungen über die ästhetische Qualität des World Trade Centers waren seit seiner Errichtung äußerst kontrovers. Die meisten Bewohner und Besucher bevorzugten das Empire State Building gegenüber der schlichten Architektur der hohen Kuben. Die Katastrophe und das veränderte Stadtbild haben das ästhetische Urteil revidiert. Hierzu hat die formale Stilisierung der Türme – zwei schlichte Rechtecke mit einem schmalen Strich für den Sendemast auf dem Nordturm – zu einer Ikone entscheidend beigetragen. Die Türme werden in den verschiedensten Varianten als Souvenirs, Devotionalien, Tätowierungen, Fenster- und Vorgartendekoration repliziert. Durch die Entfernung des konkreten Kontexts wird das Zeichen zu einer kulturellen Chiffre, in ihm verbinden sich Glauben und Stolz auf die amerikanische Nation, ein quasi re-

ligiöser Eifer mit Projektionen von Prüfung und Erlösung durch die auf sich selbst bezogenen Tugenden. Es scheint, dass Gebäude zum ersten Mal in der genuin menschlichen Rolle des Märtyrers rezipiert werden.

Eine weitere Perspektive religiöser Bildmetaphorik ergibt sich – unter der Annahme, dass die offizielle Version von den islamistischen Terroristen aus der Organisation eines Osama bin Ladens korrekt wäre –, wenn der Ikonoklasmus des Talibanregimes, etwa die Zerstörung der größten stehenden Buddhastatuen der Welt im Bamiyan Tal im März 2001, auf die Zerstörung der beiden Türme des WTC übertragen würde.

Den Hintergrund für die Gegenüberstellung (**fig. 3**, S. 11) bildet die Bezeichnung „Big Apple". Im Zuge einer Marketingmaßnahme in den 1970ern wurde Manhattan als eben jener Big Apple bezeichnet, als ironisierender Vergleich mit Babylon und der vermeintlichen Konzentration weltweiter und weltlicher Sündhaftigkeit in New York. Diese Gegenüberstellung wird abgerundet durch die Stilisierung der beiden Türme als heterosexuelles Paar und religiös konnotierte Vorstellungen und Versprechungen des Paradieses.

genuin oder kanonisch

Die Eindringlichkeit eines Ereignisses führt zu der Deklamation seiner Einmaligkeit. Zur Untersuchung dieser Hypothese ist es möglich, der Frage der genuinen Bilderzeugung nachzugehen: „Nichts wird mehr so sein wie vorher!" Gehört das Ereignis selbst aber schon zu dem „nicht mehr" oder noch zu dem „wie vorher"? Sind Ereignis und nachfolgende Reaktionen genuin oder Transformationen des Vorherigen? Entspricht die Transformation dem vermeintlich Anderen, dem Neuen?

Im Umkehrschluss der Realität entsprechen die Bilder des 11. September der kulturellen Produktion bis zu diesem Datum. Hochhaus, Flugzeug und Kinematografie sind in etwa zur selben Zeit geboren und in den letzten hundert Jahren zu den bedeutsamen Attributen einer weltweiten Zivilisation weiterentwickelt worden. Als 1945 ein amerikanischer Bomber bei schlechter Sicht in das Empire State Building flog, war das sicherlich nicht der erste Unfall dieser Art, und seit der Errichtung von Hochhäusern gehört es zu den Anforderungen an deren Konstruktion, dass sie dem Aufprall eines Flugzeuges standhalten. Flugzeugentführungen gehören spätestens seit den 1970er-Jahren zum Repertoire von Terroristen. Computerspiele und Filmindustrie versorgen ihr Publikum mit unzähligen Zerstörungsvariationen von Gebäuden und Städten. Die Bilder sind nicht neu und es scheint, dass nur die Dimension ihrer medialen Inszenierung die Eindringlichkeit determiniert.

Die Suche nach einer genuinen Bildlogik – im Vergleich mit einer geschichtlichen Einordnung und der kulturellen Rezeption von globalen Bedrohungsszenarien seit Hiroshima und episch dramatischer Katastrophen wie dem Untergang der Titanic – wird in der Betrachtung der Reaktionen fortgesetzt. Das Bild von den drei Feuerwehrleuten, die am 11. September 2001 eine amerikanische Flagge auf den rauchenden Trümmern des World Trade Centers hissen, ist das Zitat einer der populärsten Fotografien des 2. Weltkrieges in den USA, die Aufnahme von Joe Rosenfeldt nach der amerikanischen Eroberung der Pazifikinsel Iwo Jima am 23. Februar 1945 (**fig.2**, S.10). In Iwo Jima sind es Soldaten, die dieses patriotische Ritual vollziehen. Seit dem 11. September werden Feuerwehr und Polizei zu zivilen Soldaten befördert und zu Helden im alltäglichen Kampf gegen das *Böse* stilisiert. Das Bild wird zu einer Ikone, tritt in Wechselwirkung mit der Gesellschaft und wird als Ritual repliziert, dabei verliert es den Bezug zu dem konkreten Ereignis. Welches sind die neuen Bilder, die im Angesicht der „symbolischen Herausforderung" über das sich endlose wiederholende Bild von Osama bin Laden als *freundlich lächelnder Mann mit dem Bart* hinausgehen?

symbol und status

Häufig wird der Symbolbegriff in Zusammenhängen verwendet, in denen er die Begriffe Metapher, Allegorie, Zeichen oder Ikone ungenügend ersetzt. In der Betrachtung oder Interpretation eines Gegenstandes oder einer Sache als *Symbol* entsteht häufig ein Missverständnis, welches darin besteht, dass die verwendeten Attribute als genuine Wesensmerkmale desselben Gegenstandes verstanden und verwendet werden.

Ausdrücke wie „Symbol des weltweiten Kapitalismus" oder „Phallussymbol" führen in die Problematik dieser Auffassung. Wenn die Höhe eines Gebäudes hinreichend für Symbole dieser Art ist, so würde ganz Manhattan aus kapitalistischen Welthandelspenissen bestehen, angefangen bei dem Flat-Iron, dem Woolworth und dem Empire State Building, jeweils die höchsten

einleitung

We will rebuild. We're going to come out of this stronger than before, politically stronger, economically stronger. The skyline will be made whole again.
Mayor Rudi Giuliani, Sept. 2001

As a symbol of America's resolve, my administration will work with Congress, and these two leaders, to show the world that we will rebuild New York City.
President George W. Bush, Sept. 2001

wiederaufbau

Aufgrund wechselnder politischer Systeme, Kriegszerstörungen und territorialer Verschiebungen ist die Entwicklung der europäischen Städte durch fortlaufende Umbrüche und Neuanfänge gekennzeichnet. Im Gegensatz dazu befinden sich amerikanische Städte in einem Kontinuum fließender Veränderung und Fortsetzung. Nach dem 11. September steht Amerika vor der Herausforderung, auf die historische Dimension eines Ortes zu antworten, wenn auch nicht zum ersten Mal, so doch mit dem Bewusstsein unbekannter Tragweite und bedeutender Verantwortung. Die Furcht vor einer Unterbrechung der linearen Entwicklung soll durch außen- und innenpolitische Macht- und Bedrohungsszenarien kompensiert werden. Doch die viel zitierte Floskel „Nichts wird mehr so sein wie vorher!" verbreitet Unbehagen, weil Diskontinuität zu Verunsicherung führt.

Deswegen äußerten sich kurz nach dem 11. September viele amerikanische Politiker, Architekten und Stadtplaner im Sinne von George W. Bush und Rudi Giuliani und sprachen vom Wiederaufbau des World Trade Centers: „Was

immer sie nieder reißen, wir werden es wieder aufbauen", Philip Johnson – „Keinesfalls niedriger als vorher: Wir dürfen nicht klein beigeben", Peter Eisenman – „Wir brauchen neue Gebäude, die ein noch stärkeres Symbol für New York sind als jene, die dort standen", Richard Meier.

das schloss

Die Geste eines imitierenden oder gar kopierenden Wiederaufbaus von zerstörten Gebäuden wird als politisch symbolische Stellungnahme interpretiert. In der Diskussion über den Wiederaufbau des Berliner Stadtschlosses argumentieren beide Seiten mit ihrem Verständnis von Geschichte und Authentizität. Dabei werden den Befürwortern des Wiederaufbaus Revision und Restauration unter Ausblendung des letzten Jahrhunderts und ihren Gegnern eine Mahnmalmentalität und politische Emphase der letzten hundert Jahre vorgeworfen. Beiden Positionen gemeinsam ist die Konnotation von Geschichte im Sinne von Dokumentation und Erziehung. Jedoch präsentieren die einen ein historisches städtebauliches Ensemble, während die anderen ein Stadtbild im Prozess historischer Veränderungen erhalten wollen.

Der grundlegende Unterschied liegt in dem Verständnis von Stadt und Stadtbild. Einerseits eine Art *diachronisches* Stadtbild, in dem eine kulissenartige architektonische Skulptur bestimmte historische Ideen und Ideale vermittelt, und andererseits das *synchronische* Stadtbild, das die Transition dieser Vorstellungen und die Brüche der Tradition als Abbild von Funktion und Geschichte widerspiegeln möchte. Philosophisch unbestimmt bleibt es eine Frage des Geschmacks, welcher Gestaltung und Künstlichkeit, welcher Utopie man den Vorrang geben möchte.

Im Verlauf der Arbeit und des Aufenthaltes vor Ort konzentrierte sich mein Interesse auf die Bewegung und die Energie des öffentlichen Prozesses. Die Beobachtungen zeigten, dass sich in diesem frühen Stadium eine Autorität der Gemeinschaft herausgebildet hatte, die sich der Bewältigung des Ereignisses und seiner Folgen annahm. Auf der Suche nach Relevanz und Authentizität hatte ich das Gefühl, dass die öffentliche Partizipation die einzige adäquate Reaktion auf die Herausforderung darstellen könnte; auf die Herausforderung einer Situation, in der von einem „Angriff auf die zivilisierte Welt", „Terror gegen Amerika", „Kampf der Kulturen" und „Krieg gegen den internationalen Terrorismus" gesprochen wurde.

In der beispiellosen Anstrengung Tausender zeigte sich das Ringen um einen Konsens widerstrebender Interessen – und ist dieses Ringen nicht die ureigenste Form der Demokratie? Die zukünftigen Entwicklungen werden zeigen, ob es sich bei dieser sowohl politischen als auch ästhetischen Einschätzung um ein eingelöstes Versprechen oder um ein theoretisches Ideal handelt.

Diese Arbeit stellt einen Tribut an den Prozess und die Rolle der Öffentlichkeit dar. Sie ist eine Gedenkschrift, sie ist das Mahnmal eines Prozesses. Darüber hinaus bietet diese Studie Einblick in die komplizierten Strukturen und eine umfangreiche Sammlung von Informationen zu dem Prozess um die Zukunft von Ground Zero.

Nach einigen künstlerischen Arbeiten im Kontext von Öffentlichkeit, öffentlichem Raum und sozialer Skulptur schien es mir nahe liegend, mich mit der Situation in New York unter dem Arbeitsansatz einer sozialkritischen Konzeptualisierung und in dem Spannungsfeld zeitgenössischer Architektur zu beschäftigen. Die vorliegende Studie kann aufgrund der thematischen und zeitlichen Dimensionen nur als unvollkommen und vorläufig bezeichnet werden: ein Fragment in dem Gewebe kollektiver und globaler Betrachtungen.

Mein Dank gilt der Initiative NewYorkNewVisions, deren Arbeit eine zentrale Stellung in meiner Betrachtung einnimmt, nicht nur aufgrund ihrer Bedeutsamkeit, sondern auch weil ich selbst in dieser Initiative über mehrere Monate mitarbeiten durfte.

Christoph Faulhaber
Hamburg, 2002
1. Auflage

vorwort

Dies ist die überarbeitete Neuauflage des Originals aus dem Jahr 2002. Der Text wurde gekürzt und ins Englische übersetzt. Durch die zeitliche Verschiebung kommt es bei manchen Zeitformen und temporären Bezügen zu Unklarheiten, die aufgrund der historischen Verankerung des Textes aber erhalten wurden.

Aus der heutigen Perspektive zeigt sich die Notwendigkeit der Neuauflage erstens, weil das Buch einen interessanten Beitrag zu aktuellen Debatten in den Bereichen der Stadtplanung und der Gegenwartskunst darstellt, zweitens, weil es das Spektrum meiner Arbeit wie auch den zu Grunde liegenden Kunstbegriff in einem erweiterten Kontext verortet. Und drittens, weil die erste Auflage inzwischen vergriffen ist.

Vereinfachend lässt sich der Ansatz dieses Buchs auf den Punkt bringen, wenn die plötzlich entstandene Leere inmitten von Downtown Manhattan als öffentlicher Raum verstanden wird. Öffentlichkeit oder die gemeinsame räumliche und zeitliche Erfahrung einer Civitas oder Gemeinschaft wurde in den 1990er-Jahren in den voneinander unabhängigen Ansätzen des Stadtplaners Dieter Läpple und des Kunsttheoretikers Nicolas Bourriaud unter dem Begriff „Relationalität" beschrieben.

Dieter Läpple rezipierte die Schaffung eines Raums durch dessen soziale Konstruktion als *relationales Raumkonzept*, während Nicolas Bourriaud unter dem Begriff der *relationalen Ästhetik* ein umfassendes Paradigma partizipativer, kontextueller und zeitbasierter Strategien der Kunstproduktion entwickelte: Raum entsteht durch gemeinsames Handeln und die Formation des Kunstwerks manifestiert sich in diskursiven, sozialen und partizipativen Strukturen.

Dieses Buch zeigt das Potenzial und die Chancen aber auch die begrenzten Möglichkeiten dieses ethisch-ästhetischen Ansatzes.

Christoph Faulhaber
Shenzhen, 2010
2. Auflage

Ich kann mich an kein Ereignis erinnern, das mich mit solcher Gewalt getroffen hätte, wie das der Bilder vom 11. September. Für mich war es, wie für die Amerikaner, der „erste Angriff auf eigenem Boden". Doch dann verflüchtigte sich die Erfahrung ins Metaphysische, das Reden begann, die Diskussionen, die Erklärungsmuster, die Instrumentalisierung des Ereignisses und die Transposition in die Realität jedweden subjektiven Verstandes.

Die Herausforderung der Bilder evoziert die kulturelle Produktion von Bildern, die sich dieser Herausforderung stellen. Welche kulturellen und künstlerischen Strategien agieren und reagieren in diesem *horror vacui*? Welche gestalterischen und ästhetischen Konzepte für die unvermeidlich notwendige Zukunft von Ground Zero können sich in einem emotional und politisch extremisierten Klima entwickeln?

Als ich Anfang 2002 nach New York kam, standen im Mittelpunkt dieser Fragen die Vergleiche mit den Debatten in Deutschland über den Wiederaufbau und die Neubebauung der historischen Mitte Berlins: das Berliner Stadtschloss, das Denkmal für die ermordeten Juden Europas, der Potsdamer Platz und das Jüdische Museum. Und es stellte sich die Frage, wie sich dieses Ringen um Gestalt – zwischen symbolischer Form und historisch authentischer Identität – zu den Planungen eines neuen World Trade Centers in Beziehung setzen ließe.

NEW YORK NY 10047/48

Der öffentliche Prozess um den Wiederaufbau des World Trade Centers nach dem 11. September 2001

CHRISTOPH FAULHABER

KERBER

EDITION YOUNG ART